WHERE TO GO FOR HELP

Where to Go for Help

Revised and Enlarged Edition

by
WAYNE E. OATES and KIRK H. NEELY

THE WESTMINSTER PRESS
Philadelphia

ISBN 0-664-24947-7

Library of Congress Catalog Card No. 70-178183

BOOK DESIGN BY
DOROTHY ALDEN SMITH

Published by The Westminster Press ®
Philadelphia, Pennsylvania

PRINTED IN THE UNITED STATES OF AMERICA

To
Pauline and Clare

CONTENTS

FOREWORD

Valuable time can be wasted by needy people as they go up one blind alley after another seeking help. We need a record of some of the attitudes to have and of some of the places to go to obtain dependable help. Numerous requests for information by letter and in personal conferences prompted us to prepare the following pages. The frequency of particular requests guided us to select the problems discussed. The nature of some of the problems will come as a surprise to some people. However, we have touched only the edges of the kinds of difficulties that people present as well as the sources of help available to them. But in order that people may most wisely and quickly find the resources of the community at large, of the self-help literature available, of the great helping professions, and especially of the churches, we have written this book. Since its first edition in 1957 an overwhelming number of new resources for helping persons in distress have been developed. One hope we have is that in as few pages as possible, we can provide ready-reference points for the reader.

People need not only to be guided to dependable sources of help; they also need some safeguards against quacks, pulp literature, and well-meaning but unskilled persons. At the same time their own need for help requires some discipline, lest they expect too much or too little of their sources of help. Both magic and self-sufficiency are vain hopes.

This book is meant to be a handbook of ready reference for people who want to know where to obtain help, for their pastors, and for other professional people who serve them. It is in no wise complete. We should like to request the reader to help us to improve these resources by supplying any additional information not included here. The literature listed was available at the time of our writing, but the reader will need to verify the continuing availability of particular items.

Also, personal experiences of success or frustration in the use of this book will help to evaluate our effort to direct people to the places where they can go for help. Every address has been checked with national agency listings, in local telephone directories, and by personal calls. Information corrections will be appreciated.

All these resources come upon the recommendation of national agencies, the Federal Government's Department of Health, Education, and Welfare, or the personal knowledge of the authors. However, the reader is encouraged to accept personal responsibility for his own experience with each agency.

WAYNE E. OATES
2825 Lexington Road
Louisville, Kentucky   40206

KIRK H. NEELY
Ormsby Village Treatment Center
Anchorage, Kentucky   40223

The Helping Character
of the Christian Fellowship

The Christian fellowship is by its very nature a cov-
enanted group of persons who are weak, sinful, and in
need. Our awareness of our sense of need has brought us
to God in Christ. In so doing, we have met together as a
"fellowship of those overtaken in faults." Our very be-
longing to the church is a confession of our need for each
other's help in dealing with the stresses and strains, the
stumblings and fallings, the accidents and the dark difficulties that we cannot understand or accept. Therefore,
the confession of need for help on any particular problem should never set us apart or cause us to feel different
from our fellow human beings, and especially "those who
are of the household of faith." Rather, it is an affirmation
of our kinship with the whole creation that is bound up
together in the fellowship of suffering. Furthermore, it
gives the Christian community—its pastor, its leaders, its
quietest member—an opportunity to "do good to all men,
and especially to those who are of the household of
faith."

The awareness of this universality of human suffering,
on the other hand, imbues the Christian who has felt the
forgiving grace of God in Christ with a "spirit of gentle-

ness" that overcomes his tendency to reject the person in need whom he confronts. He has a spirit of tender love that is rooted in his own awareness of frailty. He himself might just as easily have had the problem troubling his brother in Christ. He considers himself also lest he too be tried by the same adversity.

But the person in need should not mistake this sense of tender love he receives from the Christian community for a sign of weakness. He should not assume that just because these people are going to be helpful, he is relieved of all responsibility for his own problem. He must afford his own willing fellowship by carrying as much of the responsibility as he can in such a way as to learn how to carry it better.

On the other hand, many people despair that anyone could be of service to them and thereby choose another way to avoid dealing with their real need. This path leads the person in need into the loneliness of self-sufficiency. He thinks more highly of himself than he ought to think. He declares a sort of "windy independence" of all men. He assumes that he can both live and die to himself. But such deification of man's own will power is really sowing to a short-lived and fleshly disappointment. A longer look, one taught by the Spirit of God, enables him to see the help of others as a means to a greater dependence upon God and as God's way of mediating this help to us. Therefore, the person in need of help should not wait until desperation pushes him frantically into the confession of his need for the service of others. As soon as he sees his basic usefulness as a person being hindered, he should seek out the rich resources of the church, the recorded experiences of others in literature, and the wider reaches of the helping professions of the community and its institutions.

In doing so, he is enabled to help others who themselves are in need. He is enheartened by the comfort wherewith God has comforted him, and by means of it he is able to comfort those who are in any affliction. He becomes an informed, enabled, and enriched person, and can lead others to the places where they too can obtain help when they need it.

Part I

THE GREAT HELPING PROFESSIONS
AND THEIR LITERATURE

1

The Great Helping Professions

A. THE CHRISTIAN MINISTRY

Our Father, to thee we confess our common sins
as ministers, for thou art our counselor too. Forgive us for our preoccupations, which keep us
from hearing the strange appeals for help all
around us. Make us faithful to hear, quick to respond, and ready to call for aid in helping all
those who are in any affliction. With the comfort
wherewith thou hast comforted us, may we become a comfort. Amen.

The time has come when people need to cease to
think of their minister as a person who *just* preaches on
Sunday. Preaching is a vital and climactic expression of
all that he has been doing in a pastoral service to his
people during the week. The late Prof. W. O. Carver, of
the Southern Baptist Theological Seminary, was once invited to come to a church with the understanding that
he would do nothing but preach to them on Sundays. He
refused, saying to them, "Unless I take the people and
their needs to heart, I cannot preach the sermons that
they need." He felt that a "load of concern to pray over
and ponder" was a necessary part of preparing to preach.

This in itself may be a kind of threat to you. You may fear that your pastor will refer to your private conversation with him in one of his public addresses. A personal request that he keep your confidence will bring home the importance of this to him. Also, you should agree not to discuss your confidences with others without letting your pastor know that you are doing so. They, and not he, may be the ones to repeat your story. On the other hand, your greatest hesitancy in going to your pastor may well lie in the fact that he is a close friend of yours and you value his time and friendship in such a way as not to want to tell him your trouble. But remember, your pastor can best express his friendship by participating privately in your deepest concerns. Do not let a shallow friendship stand in the way of the real help that a genuinely deep friendship with your pastor can afford.

1. When to Send for Your Pastor

Here is a careful list of the specific times when you should call your pastor and ask for a visit from him or for an appointment to see him in his study or home, where he can provide you with a sure measure of privacy. These times are as follows:

a. When a loved one is seriously ill and facing death.
b. When a relative continues to be despondent after the death of a loved one.
c. When you are facing a surgical operation.
d. When you face adjustment to a physical handicap.
e. When you are going through a long convalescence.
f. Following the birth of a baby.
g. When a son goes into military service.

h. When your last son or daughter has left the home and you are replanning your own life.

i. When you are planning to retire.

j. When you are thinking of changing jobs.

k. When you desire to join the church.

l. When you have begun to worry about excessive drinking or drug abuse.

m. When you are having difficulty in your marriage.

n. When a loved one is drinking excessively or misusing drugs.

o. When you are choosing a lifework and feel uncertain about your choice.

p. When you are choosing a life mate and have doubts about your choice.

q. When as a parent you are concerned about either of the two above problems for your son or daughter.

r. When you are discouraged and life has lost its meaning.

s. When a loved one has become despondent for no obvious reason.

t. When the behavior of a loved one shows marked and rapid change, whether it is toward excessive misbehavior or excessive interest in religion.

u. When you are having difficulty praying.

2. The Role of Your Minister as a Counselor in Your Personal Crises

Ministers have always been confidants of their people in the above-named intimate crises of their lives. Even though people for a while began to seek out secular counselors rather than ministers, there is good evidence that this tide has begun to turn. The military chaplain during World War II became a comrade to his men. They depended upon him for counsel in individual contacts instead of flocking to hear him as he preached to great crowds. These men came back from the war. They and their families began to look for this kind of relationship to their pastor. Chaplains came back to theological schools seeking intensive training in pastoral counseling in numbers that overwhelmed the resources of their schools.

Since World War II, the training of ministers in pastoral counseling is a normal part of their education. The intensive training is approaching a subspeciality of the ministry. The American Association of Pastoral Counselors lists 540 pastoral counselors, who are located in every part of the United States. Their names are listed in a directory available at 31 West 10th Street, New York, N.Y. 10011; tel. (212) 260-4170.

Scientific techniques of psychological and therapeutic counseling have exerted a vital influence upon the minister's interpretation of his own role in such a way that he is today likely to sense counseling needs quickly. For these reasons and many others, people apparently are turning to their ministers for personal counseling now in a way not true in former years. People find in their minister the things that make him a helpful counselor.

3. What Makes Your Minister a Helpful Counselor?

Several things characterize the minister who is a helpful counselor. He combines the strength and decisiveness of a wise father with the gentleness and understanding of a devout mother. He knows how to be both tender and firm without being inconsistent. This is what we call "the pastor's heart." It usually shows in the man's preaching, if he has it at all, and can be sensed by the distressed person more readily than by the carefree person. The way the man preaches reflects a deliberate and thoughtful wisdom. He weighs his words carefully, but once they have been weighed they are spoken with conviction.

The minister, again, who is helpful as a counselor does not give snap judgments about great life concerns. He lays the matter to heart enough to talk to you more than once, after having had time to sleep over it and to pray about it. He may consult his Bible and other books. With your permission, he may consult experts on your particular trouble before he sees you a second time.

The genuinely concerned pastoral counselor will help you to arrive at your own solutions of your problem rather than give you ready-made solutions all his own. He is like the mathematics instructor who teaches you the principles of problem-solving instead of giving you the answer from the back of the book! This takes more time. It calls for definite growth on your part, which he encourages by his experience, friendship, and maturity. Consequently, this pastor is likely to listen more than he talks. He will try to understand you more than he tries to force you to understand him and his position. This minister knows that when he gives you ready-made solutions to your problem he is depriving you of growth and making you as dependent as a child upon him. Yet he understands what loneliness is and stands by you as a "son of encouragement" until you arrive at your own maturity. On the other hand, the wise pastor will give you information that he knows you do not have. He will not keep you in the dark when he can throw a little light upon your problem.

This latter kind of information-giving is particularly important when it comes to the areas of knowledge in which the pastor is supposed to be authoritative. He can give you dependable information about the Bible, church history, Christian ethics, Christian doctrine, and church practices. He can lead you to dependable sources of further information. This is particularly necessary if you or a loved one contemplate marrying a person of a quite different religious faith. If your pastor cannot give you authentic information, the two of you can learn together as you seek the truth.

A helpful pastoral counselor does not try to be an authority on everything. He knows his limitations and both knows how and is not ashamed to call upon the help of other skilled persons such as doctors, lawyers, teachers, and businessmen for the most help that his community can afford you in meeting your problem satisfactorily.

The genuinely helpful pastoral counselor is not afraid of you. If you demand of him things that are not for your own best good, he is not afraid to refuse what you demand. If you ask him to give you a final answer on a problem for which the only satisfactory answer is the one you and he work out together through suffering and effort, he will gently get this fact across to you without driving you away. If you demand that he "barge in" uninvited upon some loved one of yours, he may tactfully refuse to do so. If you threaten him with trouble in the church if he does not conform to your demands, he is still not afraid of you and will continue to respond to your real rather than your imagined needs.

Obviously, then, the effective pastoral counselor depends heavily upon the leadership of the Holy Spirit and does not grieve or run ahead of him. This makes of the pastor a man of good report, able, and filled with the Holy Spirit. A third Presence is apparent in his counseling with you. The pastor takes his place as a fellow sinner and sufferer and seeker with you. His access to God enables you with him to overcome sin, pain, and confusion.

Finally, the pastor is the faithful person who, representing the church, is *there* when you need him. He symbolizes the whole church, and in a real sense the church is there in his person.

B. THE MEDICAL PROFESSION

We praise thee, O God, for our friends, the doctors and nurses, who seek the healing of our bodies. We bless thee for their gentleness and patience, for their knowledge and skill. We remember the hours of our suffering when they brought relief, and the days of our fear and anguish at the bedside of our dear ones when they came as ministers of God to save the life thou hadst given. May we reward their fidelity and devotion by our loving gratitude, and do thou uphold them by the satisfaction of work well done. Amen.   (*Walter Rauschenbusch.*)

1. Finding a Physician

The key person in any medical-help program of an individual, a family, or a group is the family physician, the *general practitioner*. He knows the family as a unit. Therefore, upon going to a new community you should, before a medical emergency arises, establish personal acquaintance with a general physician. A good way to do this is for the breadwinner of the family to go to him for a general checkup, a thing that every person should do periodically anyhow. Your doctor will thus have a clinical record of at least one member of the family, and can gradually become acquainted with the other members of the family as need arises. A general physician often serves as a confidential person with whom you can talk about things that you might be embarrassed to talk over with others. Furthermore, when you need more specialized medical services, he can usually refer you to those persons whose ability he has seen demonstrated. In the long run he can save you money that you might spend going from one specialist to another on the basis of your misinterpretation of your own symptoms. *Remember: you are your own poorest diagnostician.*

When you seek the aid of specialists, then, it is best to go through your family physician. If, however, after much searching about, you find that you are becoming more and more confused by the multitude of medical opinions, it may be well to go to a medical-school setup. You may go through either their *private* diagnostic clinic or their *public* diagnostic clinic. A private diagnostic service is usually given by the medical staff of senior physicians, medical-school faculty members, etc. The cost of this kind of service is somewhat higher than that of the public diagnostic clinic. The outpatient or public clinic is under the rigid supervision of the medical faculty. But the actual work-up of your case is done by interns and residents who are in the final stages of their training. Some people shy away from being "practiced on," but in a very real way the less experienced doctor will be all the more cautious to move slowly and pains-takingly with you. The findings of the less experienced doctor are checked at every point by seasoned physicians. Therefore the care you get is doubled. Such clinics have diagnostic equipment for testing, for making X rays, etc., that is not available to the average general practitioner. Working conditions are strictly controlled. Clinics also possess the added advantage of having many different doctors working in close, correlated consultation with one another, pooling their results and coming to a collabo-rated conclusion.

Specialists of every kind have developed within mod-ern medicine. For instance, when a new baby is expected at your house, you will do well to get the services of a good *obstetrician* in addition to those of your general practitioner. Often an obstetrician is also a *gynecologist,* a person who specializes not only in the art and science of assisting in the prenatal care and delivery of children but also in the whole gamut of female needs for medical hygiene and therapy. Such a person should be called upon to give the bride a premarital examination in order to assess any problems that she may encounter in bear-ing children in marriage. A gynecologist can also prepare the bride for unhindered effectiveness in the sexual re-lationships of marriage. Furthermore, he can advise her authoritatively on the use of birth-control measures and, if she so desires, fit her with a diaphragm, prescribe vagi-nal jellies, foams, douches, etc. Diaphragms should al-ways be prescribed by a specialist in gynecology. Pre-scriptions for oral contraceptives ("the pill") can be written on the basis of the individual patient's medical history. Oral contraceptives should be prescribed only after a careful history has been taken and a diagnosis of the individual's health is made.

Another specialist who is the standby of the family is the *pediatrician*, or the child specialist. You will find that such a doctor is a general physician for your children, knowing the variations that diseases manifest in children. Problems such as eating difficulties, bed-wetting, masturbation, thumb-sucking, temper tantrums, sex information for children, childhood phobias, and resistance to going to school are garden varieties of problems with children that parents tend to worry either too much or too little about. A good pediatrician can help you inexpensively with these. The security of your children's physical and emotional health is increased beyond measure by a pediatrician's constant supervision. Your general physician can help you find him.

A *surgeon* can also be found, when the necessity arises, by consultation with your general physician. Surgery is a radical measure of therapy and has saved countless lives. But because it is a radical measure, it should be done only upon the advice of both a general family physician and a surgeon in consultation with each other. The reason for this is that the family physician is usually aware of the total family situation, the history of the other illnesses of the patient, and he has a more leisurely relationship to the patient as a person. Furthermore, as the proverb puts it, "two heads are better than one" in such issues.

A *psychiatrist* is another specialist in the medical field. Bear in mind that a psychiatrist is always an M.D. He is never called a "consulting psychologist," or a "counselor," but is always listed as a physician. Therefore, both your minister and your family physician can help you in the decision as to whether your problem merits psychiatric attention. If your minister is trained as he should be, he

THE GREAT HELPING PROFESSIONS

will have some knowledge of the early signs of mental illness. Thus he can collaborate with your family physician in protecting you or your loved ones from embarrassment, and in helping you to get early treatment. He can be a genuine friend to you during treatment and when you go back into your normal routine of life after treatment. Your minister should consult with your family physician, and you will enable him to help you more if you will either suggest this to him or give him the permission to talk with your physician if he asks for it.

Comprehensive mental health centers are available for psychiatric consultation. The exact locations, telephone numbers, and services of these centers can be found in the Mental Health Directory published by the National Institute of Mental Health, 5454 Wisconsin Avenue, Chevy Chase, Md. 20015. These agencies concentrate on such areas as alcoholism, drug abuse, suicide prevention, mental disorders, delinquency, and child and family mental health. Increasingly within the next few months and years cities of even modest size will have central child-care referral agencies, suicide prevention centers, crisis control centers, poison control centers, rumor control centers, etc.

Emotional illness, mental disorders, or whatever you have learned to call personal problems that have grown to uncontrollable proportions, are like any other illness. They are most easily treated in their early stages. The recovery rate is highest with persons who seek treatment earliest. The chronic illness is usually apparent in the person who wasted valuable treatment time in arguing with himself and his loved ones, and in experiencing one failure after another before he admitted that he needed help.

Your general physician, especially if he has studied

medicine in the last twenty-five years, has received a measure of training in psychiatry. He can help you with simple emotional disturbances, and can alert you as to the impending possibility of the need for psychiatric attention. The need for a psychiatrist and other more highly specialized medical problems will be discussed in detail later in these pages. These are general observations that apply to securing medical help.

2. Finding a Nurse

A very important person in your need for medical help is the nurse. Nursing care can be obtained at several different levels of your need. First, even if you are in a more remote rural area, you should by all means know your *public-health nurse*. Usually she is connected with your county Board of Health. There are 21,000 public-health nurses throughout the United States at work in all areas of health. They help the handicapped to gain health, give bedside care to the sick at home, assist expectant mothers, teach practices for maintaining good health, protect sanitation, and control communicable diseases in schools, industry, and farming. Only 13 percent of the pay of the public-health nurse comes from the people she serves. Families able to do so pay the full cost of her visit, others pay what they can. To those who can pay nothing, free service is given.

The *Visiting Nurse Association* is another important agency to which to turn for nursing help, especially if it is for bedside nursing care for persons who are ill at home. Registered professional nurses go into the home to give whatever nursing care the doctor prescribes. Not only nursing service is available through the Visiting

Nurse Association but also such paramedical workers as home health aides, physical therapists, speech therapists, medical social workers, and mobile meal suppliers. Fees are exceptionally reasonable, and social service attention can help to get public assistance coverage for those unable to pay. The length of the visit is limited to the time needed to give the prescribed care. However, fees are adjusted to family income and to account for special appointments and for visits of more than one hour. This part-time service is ideally suited for persons who either do not need or cannot afford full-time nursing care at home.

In our own community too, the Visiting Nurse Association is a voluntary, nonprofit agency. Its funds come from patients' fees, United Fund, and other contributions. Anyone ill at home and living in our county may have its services. The agency gives care to persons who pay the full fee charged for a visit, to those who can pay only a part of the fee, and to those who cannot pay anything. This care must be arranged for in advance. The boon these skilled professional visitants can bring to an overburdened housewife in the earlier hours of the day in helping to administer baths, treatments, etc., to home-cared-for patients is difficult to overestimate. The giving of hypodermics, dressing of surgical wounds, irrigation of bladder and bowel, and giving of specific instructions to the family—all these and many more are types of service rendered. This agency is usually listed in your telephone book under "Visiting Nurse Association," or may be contacted through your state Board of Health. It may be listed as a "Home Health Service." There are approximately 3,000 such agencies in this country.

The question will be asked as to how to find a *private*

nurse for a period of time. The need may be for a practical nurse or for a registered nurse. The best way is to look in your telephone directory for the "Nurses' Registry," the "Nurses' Service Bureau," or a similar title. Names of these organizations may vary a bit locally. If you cannot find such a listing, you should call the director of nurses at the nearest hospital. She will be able to assist you, or to give you the exact local telephone number you should call.

3. Hospitalization

Going to a hospital is a part of the normal existence of increasing numbers of persons in the maintenance of health, and not just a clutching struggle with disease. There are three types of hospitals: the state-, city-, or county-owned hospital, the federal hospital, and the private hospital. In brief, there are public hospitals and private hospitals. But the uses that hospitals can be put to vary widely in terms of whether or not they are operated by the government, especially at the point of support.

The county and state Boards of Health usually operate public general medical and surgical hospitals, which in turn usually have a service for psychiatric patients on a short-term basis. State governments tend to operate hospitals for long-term, chronic illnesses—for example, hospitals for tuberculosis patients, and hospitals for chronic mental patients and for the short-term care of mental patients in areas where there are no city or county facilities. With the appropriation of federal funds at the local community level, more and more communities are building municipal and county hospitals. These are set up in such a way that hospitalization is more and more within the reach of even the poorest person.

The functions of a state and/or county Board of Health are wider than that of hospitalization, embracing the dental health and education of the populace, the fight against chronic diseases such as cancer, heart disease, diabetes, and arthritis. The great epidemic diseases, such as polio and typhoid, are their province to study and control. Venereal disease control, treatment, and education are functions of the boards of health, and industrial health and accident attention concerns boards of health vitally. Naturally, well-baby clinics, maternal health, environmental sanitation, restaurant inspection, and meat and milk inspection consume the time and energy of these public-health servants, offering protection from many things that formerly went under the names of demons and evil spirits. Theirs is truly a religious ministry that calls for the prayerful gratitude of the whole community. Difficulty with any of the above-named problems can be met by calling the Board of Health.

Federal hospitalization has been provided for along several lines. The Veterans Administration hospitals have all types of hospital care for eligible persons. These institutions can be reached through the Veterans Administration representatives in your county-seat town. The Federal Government also provides at least two types of specialized care through the United States Public Health Service. For instance, the victims of Hansen's disease, or leprosy, as it is popularly known, can get hospital care at the U.S. Public Health Hospital at Carville, Louisiana. (NOTE: A Protestant agency for the care of lepers is The American Leprosy Missions, Inc., with central offices at

297 Park Avenue, South, New York, N.Y. 10017.) Victims of drug addiction also have special needs, for which the National Institute of Mental Health maintains hospitals in Lexington, Kentucky, and Fort Worth, Texas. An ensuing chapter deals in detail with other resources for the care of drug abuse and addiction cases.

4. The Cost of Medical Care

Economic anxiety grips you when you think of medical care. It means additional bills. It may mean an interruption of your work, a curtailing of your earning power. Of course, hospitalization insurance is one of the surest ways of distributing your medical bills over a long period of time and of having them cost you less. Plans such as Blue Cross and Blue Shield, and other types of insurance, provide inexpensive buffers against heavy medical costs.

The Social Security insurance of the Federal Government has extensive sick-leave coverage for persons participating in this program. The employer of a worker can, through his personnel office, give the employee specific asistance and advice on this resource. Consultation with the local office of the U.S. Department of Health, Education, and Welfare will give further help in tapping these resources. The Medicare and Medicaid programs of the Federal Government are available in addition to Old Age Assistance for sick persons over the age of sixty-five.

One final thing about medical costs needs to be said: *Decreased efficiency because of poor health is often more expensive than medical care in that earning power is reduced.* We remember a man who was suffering from a severe depression at midlife who did not feel that he could afford psychiatric help. He was under the illusion that this kind of care is more expensive than the total cost of other kinds of serious medical help. Therefore, he was hindered in his work for many weeks before he went to a doctor. He recovered rapidly and saw that he had been taking the most expensive route without medical care. In the scope of two or three weeks he was back on his job, earning his livelihood rather than being dependent upon anyone for it.

C. THE LEGAL PROFESSION

O Thou who didst bring order out of chaos and create an ordered universe, we thank thee for those who help us to understand human law and the patterns of legal relationships. We pray for all lawyers, that theirs may be a search for thy justice in our behalf. In the name of him who sums up the Law and the Prophets, Jesus Christ our Lord, we pray. Amen.

One of the main themes of this book is that the best way to meet a need for help is to anticipate the need before it arises. This is especially true of the need for legal help. Most honest folk never run into criminal law, although they are often the victims of confidence games, sales rackets, frame-ups, and mistaken identity. Then, too, we may as well acknowledge that people of respectable families furnish their quota to the ranks of crime: manslaughter, embezzlement, tax evasion, etc. As Kathryn Close has said, however, "The law is a friend, not an enemy, but a friend that is not fully available without a lawyer" (Kathryn Close, *Do You Need a Lawyer?* p. 2;

Public Affairs Pamphlet No. 205). Expert guidance is necessary to secure legal rights and protect your investments, relationships, and property.

Here are some of the recurrent problems you may encounter that call for legal advice:

a. Automobile accidents, and other types of accidents.
b. Clear deed and title to home ownership.
c. Adoption of a child.
d. Legal guardianship.
e. Probation of a will or administration of an estate.
f. The making of a will.
g. Landlord and tenant disputes.
h. Defective material in installment buying.
i. Zoning regulation as to disputed use of your property.
j. Legal separations or divorce.
k. Child support disputes.

1. Hindrances to Finding Adequate Legal Help

One of the most effective barriers to finding adequate legal help is your assumption that you are an exception to such needs, that nothing requiring legal aid could happen to you. But the law is impersonal and applies to everybody. A personally chosen lawyer brings the law out of the realm of the impersonal and enables it to meet your specific needs. Another hindrance to your getting legal help when you need it is your fear of lawyers, that they are "dishonest" and want to charge you exorbitant fees. But these are what we call "stereotyped" ideas, arising out of idle rumor, radio and television whodunits, and the relatively few shysters who latch onto every great helping profession. Do not let popular generalizations such as these create in you a false sense of confidence that you are your own best lawyer in a difficult legal problem. Most of us are not ordinarily so. Probably the most common hindrance to your getting legal help is procrastination. You simply do not have your real estate titles looked up and insured, and the like. These are things that stay put until they blow up. Your procrastination diverts you to other things that seem to be more pressing at a given moment.

The prospective client of a lawyer should be aware of *the code of ethics among reputable lawyers*. This code in itself places the initiative on the client to find the help of the lawyer. The code taboos any lawyer who goes out searching for clients, popularly known as "ambulance chasing." Advertising is strictly forbidden. Signs identifying the office of a lawyer can be only a certain, rather inconspicuous size. The lawyer accepts several obligations upon having established contact with and pledged his services to the client. He respects the confidences entrusted to him. He is prohibited from representing conflicting sides of a legal issue. He is forbidden to receive money from the opponent of his client. He accepts it as a duty to settle a matter out of court whenever it is to his client's interest. He refuses to create legal situations in order to get clients. His major positive function is to advise his client in a way that will keep legal services except for advice from being needed. (Kathryn Close, *ibid.*)

2. Finding a Lawyer in a Rural or Small-Town Community

This is not nearly so difficult as it is in a larger, more impersonal city. In any instance, however, it is not the wisest thing simply to pick up a telephone book and call the first person listed under "Attorneys" in the yellow pages. The American Bar Association has taken some specific steps to help you get together with reputable attorneys when you need them. This is done through what is known as *Lawyer Referral Services*. They are sometimes called "Legal Registries" or "Lawyers' Reference Plans." "Through centrally located offices run by legally trained directors, they offer the lawyer a place to register his willingness to accept clients on a moderate-fee basis, and offer the client a safe channel for reaching the lawyer." (*Ibid.*, p. 14.) These services are usually listed under one of the above titles in your telephone directory. If not, the long-distance operator can locate the service in the nearest larger city.

For persons unable to pay for legal services, the Legal Aid Society plan has been devised in most larger communities and even in many smaller county-seat towns. First located in 1876 in New York City, these agencies are now to be found in cities and counties throughout the country. These societies limit their services to people who are legally involved in civil cases. Often they are subsidized by charitable agencies of the community, and they very carefully protect themselves from being exploited by persons who are perfectly capable of paying for services.

The law provides that the court can assign legal assistance to a person, but usually this assistance gets to the client too late and under hurried conditions. Too often this kind of help is given under conditions contributing to carelessness and without much real motivation on the part of the lawyers assigned. A better service is the Public Defender Plan in use in such towns as Memphis, Tennessee, and Los Angeles, California, and in states such as Rhode Island. Here the office is equipped with a full-time trial and investigating staff, which aggressively seeks out the persons who are without adequate legal defense. This aid is for people involved in criminal cases. Furthermore, when all these resources in the search for legal assistance fail, you can "start over" in your search by calling the law school nearest you, which is often associated with a university. These men are teachers, "know the territory," and can guide you to a lawyer.

One final suggestion: If none of these thoughts answer your need, the most helpful suggestion we could make is that you seek out your own pastor and ask his aid in finding a dependable lawyer. In your own church membership you may find dedicated Christian men and women who are trained in the law. They will be glad for the opportunity to express their Christian witness through the medium of their profession.

D. THE TEACHING PROFESSION

We give thanks unto thee, O God, for the teachers who have inspired us and who join with parents in the guidance and instruction of children. We pray for an increased awareness of the size of their great responsibilities. Forgive us when we expect too much of them and when we overlook

what they can do for us. Give them a sense of
continually serving thee in what they are doing in
order that their relationship to thee may shine
through the works of their hands. In the name of
the great Teacher, we pray. Amen.

Parents, children, pastors, churches—all of us tend to
take our public-school teachers for granted when it
comes to turning to them for specialized help on specific
problems. The bane of overspecialization has fallen least
heavily on public-school teachers. They are expected to
know more specific information about a larger number of
subjects than most of the trained people of their community. The laws of the states, furthermore, are written
in most instances in a way that requires that teachers
continue their education if they are to keep their place of
responsibility and if they are to continue to earn pay
raises. This should be expected of all professions. It is
legally required of the teacher.

More than this, being a public-school teacher calls for
a deep sense of personal dedication. Teachers are not
paid commensurately with persons of other professions
of similar or equal training. They really must have a
sense of mission to stick with teaching for such low pay.

The public-school teacher is a vitally necessary resource person in helping you in the early stages of difficulty with your school-age children. A child's trouble
may show itself first in the classroom situation. Often the
teacher can give you the insight that only an outsider
can give. He or she is trained in the basic essentials of
child psychology, developmental psychology, and the
psychology of learning. Furthermore, a teacher knows
many of the resources of the community and can lead
you to other helpful persons.

Rural families, in particular, need to pay close attention to the services the schoolteacher can offer them. The home-demonstration agents, the county agents, the 4-H club workers, and the public-school system are all closely tied in with the ongoing life of the rural community. Skilled persons in these groups are at the grass roots of human need. They are within reach of the most remote areas of the country.

Furthermore, public-school teachers are related to other educators all over the country, foremost among whom are college and university faculties and administrations. Specialists of every conceivable kind are working in teaching and research in the institutions of higher learning. For instance, *psychologists* are usually affiliated with a college or university, although they may spend their time almost wholly in a hospital or clinic setting. Research and teaching are at the heart of their concern. They can be of especial aid in the use of clinical tests and the vocational guidance of young people, particularly those who are exceptional for any reason. They can render intensive counseling aid through the psychological clinic of their school. In a few parts of the country, New York City in particular, psychologists are working as private psychotherapists. This is an emerging trend. However, they are usually connected with a school or hospital in a teaching-research role. *Personal guidance counselors* in both high school and college settings can offer real help to parents and children, especially in the effort to adapt the educational program of the child to the vocational goals of his life.

E. THE SOCIAL-WORK PROFESSION

At the crossing of the crowded ways of life, our
Father, we meet the social workers ministering to
human need. May we through our prayers and
understanding find that comradeship with them
which will sustain them in a sure sense of thy purpose for their good deeds. Establish the works of
their hands, and may thy beauty rest upon them.
In the name of him who worked thy works while
it was day, we pray. Amen.

Trained social workers have come into their own as
counselors. Many work within the context of some kind
of clinic, agency, or institution. Rarely do they work in
private practice as counselors. Usually they have at least
a master's degree from a qualified school of social work
such as the universities of our country are sponsoring.
An increasing number are equipped with a doctoral degree.

The trained social worker is able to help you with a
variety of problems. The *psychiatric social worker* can
give you real preliminary help in thinking through the
need for psychiatric help for yourself and/or your loved
ones. You will find the psychiatric social worker in your
local mental hygiene clinic, child-guidance clinic, the
outpatient department of the psychiatric service of your
tax-supported city or state hospitals, and more recently
on the staffs of comprehensive mental health centers all
over the United States. The *medical social service* in
your local, city, county, or Veterans Administration hospital can guide you with reference to the financial, family, and other complications that arise when you or your

loved ones are hospitalized for medical or surgical reasons. Then, again, social workers are intensely involved in helping families who have children with *specialized difficulties*. Social workers are related to orphanages, maternity homes, adoption agencies, delinquency institutions, and other agencies set up to care for children. If you come into contact with any of these institutions, ask for the social service department.

The welfare departments of federal, state, county, and city governments employ social workers for a wide variety of specialized services that these governments provide on a public-assistance basis. The routine services offered by the Social Security Act of the Federal Government, for instance, can be received by going to the local office of the Social Security Administration or by contacting them through your employer. The more recent resources of the agency afford *aid to disabled adults*. This program is administered locally through social-work investigation. Write for the pamphlet *Financial Assistance Programs for the Handicapped,* National Institute for Mental Health, Office of Information, Bethesda, Md. 20014.

Another service made available to you by the Federal Government through social workers is *vocational rehabilitation for civilians*. Medical service, counsel and guidance, and job-training and job-finding are all concerns of theirs. By writing to the U.S. Department of Health, Education, and Welfare, to the Office of Vocational Rehabilitation, or by consulting your local welfare office, you can get information as to your eligibility for such services.

Probably the most extensive services are the direct public-assistance programs of the Federal Government in cooperation with state, county, and city governments. These include aid to dependent families, aid to dependent children, aid to dependent aged, and aid to dependent blind. Your local welfare workers, trained in social work, are the persons who administer these programs of assistance. Your local welfare office can give you specific guidance if you think you are in any one of these groups.

F. THE CLINICAL PSYCHOLOGIST

We give thee thanks, O God, for clinical psychologists, thy servants sent forth to bring peace to the restless and good news to the afflicted, to bind up the brokenhearted and to proclaim liberty to those who are captive. Be thou their guide as these our fellow ministers seek in a spirit of gentleness to restore unity to the souls under their care. Through their work may the mind of Jesus Christ become the focus of our identity. He is the Lord of us all. Amen.

There was a time when psychology was confined largely to the classroom or to the research laboratory. This is no longer the case. The clinical psychologist today is often engaged in direct service to individuals, families, and groups as well as in teaching and research. His training involves intensive clinical experience in various forms of psychotherapy, behavior modification, and counseling in relation to his psychological examinations of persons through the use of diagnostic tests.

The clinical psychologists today spend considerable time in the treatment of small children for learning disorders, behavior disorders, and phobic difficulties. They are becoming increasingly useful to middle and later adolescents who are trying to assess their abilities and plan their school work in senior high school and in the early years of college. One of the most common examples of their ministry is the so-called under-achiever, that is, the young person with bright to brilliant intelligence who consistently does poor schoolwork. Another kind of problem among some late adolescents is the compulsion for perfectionism. A student may be unable to accept anything but perfection in his schoolwork. Prompt and careful attention by a clinical psychologist may prevent later trouble.

Clinical psychologists today are also pioneering in different forms of group work, such as reality therapy, transactional analysis, and various forms of reeducation treatment. They are especially adept in working with some of the "unlearning" of the bad habits that people develop.

Clinical psychologists can be found on the staffs of psychological clinics at universities. Comprehensive mental health centers have them on their staffs. They are often listed as associates of a group of psychiatrists, or can be reached through your family physician, pediatrician, or pastor.

2

The Main Principles
of Obtaining Help

> We bring before thee, O Lord, the troubles and
> perils of peoples and nations, the sighing of pris-
> oners and captives, the sorrows of the bereaved,
> the necessities of strangers, the helplessness of the
> weak, the despondency of the weary, the failing
> powers of the aged. O Lord, draw near to each,
> for the sake of Jesus Christ our Lord. (*Anselm.*)

A. HOW TO SELECT A COUNSELOR

The foundation upon which any really helpful relationship is established is confidence and trust. How can
you measure a given person—a minister, a doctor, a lawyer, a businessman, a friend, or a neighbor—to find out
whether he or she would be a dependable and trustworthy counselor? Let us suggest a few criteria. No one
of these taken singly is wholly valid unless qualified by
all the others.

1. Who Sponsors Your Counselor?

Is your counselor sponsored by a permanent and recognized institution or agency in your community? For

instance, if you are looking for a medical doctor, a member of the staff of the hospital you would choose if you were going to be hospitalized is usually a dependable and trustworthy choice. Therefore, if you are in a strange community, you might profit by calling the superintendent of the hospital of your denomination, or the supervisor of nursing in that hospital or in another hospital of the community.

Or, for instance, ministers can be evaluated as to their trustworthiness in terms of the churches that sponsor them. This is one of the reasons why a person more often can turn with trust to his pastor than to free-lance preachers. The established pastor has been put under trust to the whole community. His measures are likely to be more cautious, but this caution is for your sake as well as for his. This is not a sure guide to dependability, but taken with other guides it is one index. If you are considering going to a pastoral counseling service, inquire who sponsors the services, whether a given congregation, a denomination, a council of churches, or an interfaith board of directors.

2. Has the Person Been in the Community Very Long?

The longer a person has been in a community, the more likely he is to have been tested by the community and entrusted with more and more responsibility. He is apt to be a busy person, because more demands are made upon him for his time. However, he is almost certain to know other qualified persons whom he can recommend to you. If you do get his own services, this person may be the more experienced counselor for having dealt with many persons' needs for help. On the other hand, occasionally busy professional people begin to depend a little too heavily on their experience and take too many shortcuts. This you want to bear in mind when you reject a younger, less experienced, but more recently trained and less hurried person. Yet an older and more experienced person can be very helpful in guiding you and in recommending to you a younger professional colleague of his.

3. Has the Person Been Adequately Trained for His Task?

The counselor's basic educational equipment should be one of the measuring rods used as you choose his services. This is particularly important in fields of service such as medicine, the law, the ministry, the psychological sciences. For instance, it is not always a safe procedure merely to look in the yellow pages of your telephone book and call a specialist listed under the appropriate title. A gynecologist, a specialist who treats the medical needs of women, their diseases and their hygiene, must have an M.D. degree and must have passed specialization board examinations and residency requirements in both obstetrics and gynecology. A psychiatrist must also have an M.D. degree, must have served a supervised residency in an approved center for psychiatric training, and must have passed a board examination of the American Psychiatric Association. A psychoanalyst must have had all this training, and in addition to this must have undergone a two- to three-year analysis of his or her own emotional adjustment to life. A psychologist should have at least an M.A. degree and preferably a Ph.D. degree.

A social worker should have a Master of Science in social work. For a directory of qualified social workers or for information concerning someone in your area, you can write to the National Association of Social Workers, 2 Park Place, New York, N.Y. 10016.

One of the best ways of checking on the training of a specialist is to ask your known and trusted family physician to look up the specialist's qualifications in a registry that doctors have, which lists those approved all over the United States. Another way is to write to your state Board of Health. Even another way is to write to the American Medical Association, 535 North Dearborn Street, Chicago, Ill. 60610. You can obtain specific advice about the training qualifications of these specialists by writing to the central office of the association to which each belongs. For instance, the address of the American Psychiatric Association is 1700 18th Street, N.W., Washington, D.C. 20009. If you yourself have some hesitancy or are inexperienced in writing such letters, your pastor and his associates can write for you.

Another field in which the training of the counselor is of great importance is that of psychological counseling. One of the main differences between a psychiatrist and a psychologist is that the psychiatrist is *always* a medical doctor, having been trained in a medical school and in a hospital. He is legally responsible for the life of his patient, and he has been legally licensed to dispense drugs and to recommend and admit patients to hospitals. The psychologist, on the other hand, has a Ph.D. from a university department of psychology, which usually requires four years of graduate training beyond the basic liberal arts degree. In addition to having a Ph.D., he should also have been approved by the American Psychological

Association. Persons wanting to know the official stand-
ing of a given counselor can find out by writing to the
American Psychological Association, 1200 17th Street,
N.W., Washington, D.C. 20036.

The choice of a minister as a counselor should also be
determined somewhat by his training in addition to the
other factors that cause people to have confidence in
their minister. A minister should have at least a Master
of Divinity degree or its equivalent, which consists of
three years of intensive theological education beyond the
basic college degree. He should have either this or a
Doctor of Ministries degree. He is more likely to be a
good personal counselor if his seminary is one in which
pastoral care, personal counseling, and clinical pastoral
training are included. You have a right to a pastor who
has something more than just good intentions in his
equipment as a counselor. You have a right to expect
that he has taken time and effort to get the kind of training that will make him more proficient in dealing with
the darker concerns of your life. You and your church do
well to encourage him by considering such training a
part of his work and by giving him opportunity to get it
if he does not have it.

(NOTE: The most definitive statement yet published
of the role, function, and training of each of the major
helping professions is to be found in the publication by
the New York Academy of Sciences entitled *Psychotherapy and Counseling*, edited by Roy Waldo Miner; 1955.
This has been published in the *Annals of the New York
Academy of Sciences*, Vol. 63, Art. 3, pp. 319–432.)

4. Is the Counselor a Person of Basic Spiritual Integrity?

A person of basic spiritual integrity is one who is morally sound, consistently honest, free from corrupting influences and practices, and strict in the fulfillment of his contracts. He has the moral grandeur of an independent spirit, thinks his own thoughts before God, and has an inherent respect for the sacredness of your personality. He treats you as a person in your own right, and not as means to his own ends. This is the kind of person whom you want as a counselor. Naturally, such a person is likely to be one with whom you will feel most at home if he is from the same spiritual community as the one to which you belong. But, on the other hand, many may often miss the real help that a person of genuine integrity and good skills has to offer because they insist upon selecting a counselor from their own religious group.

Many professional persons will be somewhat reluctant to make any show at all of their religious persuasion for two reasons, i.e., they do not want people to feel that they are using religion in order to get patients or counselees, and they do not want those who are not necessarily religious or who are of a religious persuasion other than their own to hesitate to come to them freely, apart from religious factors in the caring relationship. But the elements of a spiritual integrity, such as have been noted here, tend to show through all such distinctions. You should look for this when you need help. Your confidence and trust, upon which a counselor will stand, is indispensable as he helps you. Without this, any suspicion or distrust on your part will hinder the usefulness of the helping person.

5. Has the Counselor Been Reasonably Successful in Dealing with the Problems of Others?

Richard Cabot, late professor at Harvard Medical School, on one occasion was asked, "How do you get patients to come to you for treatment?" His reply was, "Treat the ones who do come successfully." The hidden wisdom is that those who are treated well will encourage others to come. The word tends to get around on "the grapevine" as to who can be most helpful and who is least helpful. This is one dependable criterion of his usefulness to you. Some of the best data you can find about a counselor will be from people who have received that counselor's services.

6. Does This Person Promise Much and Do Little, or Does He Promise Little and Do Much?

One real indication of a quack is the extravagance of his claims. He makes large promises of how absolutely certain he is that he can succeed where all others have failed. In doing so, he is likely to resort to two unsavory practices. He may "run down" other counselors, saying all manner of evil against them as he builds himself up. Or he may resort to various types of heavy advertising on radio, television, in the newspaper, etc.

To the contrary, the dependable and trustworthy counselor is likely to be very conservative in what he promises, but actually accomplishes more in the long run. He usually makes few comments in the earlier contacts with you, because he is diligently studying your situation. Therefore, do not wait until the last minute and run to him expecting instant magic from him. Rather, go to him expecting him to take some time with you if your problems are of any serious proportion at all. He will studiously join with you in seeking to develop a fellowship in which both of you understand your situation better together through the process of talking things out. He will walk along with you, and your perspective will change from time to time as you confer with him about your growing insight. In this encounter, the prayerful concern of a patient counselor becomes more than mere advice. The dedicated spirit of seeking that he teaches you will mean more than a basketful of flowery promises or a set of "pat" answers that amount to clichés.

7. Can You Trust This Person Basically?

This question reflects something about both you and your counselor. You may be fundamentally suspicious, and your capacity to trust anyone may be at a low ebb. This may be for the real reason of having been hurt often. On the other hand, you may be judging and condemning a person before you have given him a trial. Or you may know that this person has not been careful in his handling of the confidences of those who went to him when they needed help. If, however, you yourself learn to overcome your fear of trusting people through the process of learning to trust a counselor, the whole venture has been one of real spiritual growth for you. You may be sure that the skilled counselor understands this. He is a minister of reconciliation enabling you to express whatever feelings or misgivings you may have. But in the final analysis, trust is a basic ingredient of all help-ing relationships.

B. HOW TO SELECT HELPFUL LITERATURE

Books are no substitute for the personal help of a wise counselor. They are valuable aids, however, in giving specific information, providing authoritative reas-surance, and developing a measure of intellectual insight into and interpretation of what is going on in your life. Life does go on, and people do read books to find an enduring and useful interpretation of their experience. Books, in a very real way, are extensions of the selfhood of an author. Read them to get acquainted with him as a person, because the trustworthy author is usually try-ing to get through to you as his reader, to hold your attention, and to stimulate your need to finish reading what he has to say. If you can feel that he is "speaking to your condition," and that he is actually "getting through" to where you really are, then you may be genuinely helped through his writing.

1. What Do the Reviewers Say?

Read book reviews that have been written by depend-able people in your own community as a guide to the selection of books. Your local newspaper, your denomi-national weekly or monthly, magazines such as *Parents' Magazine, The Christian Century,* and others will help you with this. *The New York Times* publishes a highly valuable book review section in each Sunday edition. Whole issues and special sections also are devoted to surveys of different subjects. For instance, one special section on children's literature appears annually, and another on religious books. The *Saturday Review* is a weekly magazine that evaluates current literature and related subjects. These resources can be found in most libraries. The popular magazines such as *Life, Time, Newsweek,* the *U.S. News & World Report,* and *The New Yorker* often have very complete and informative reviews.

2. Consult Your Local Librarian

For advice as to the value of a given book, your librarian is a "quiet teacher." He or she usually does not make speeches or hold classes, but in the quietness of the reading rooms and among the bookshelves of the library guides eager minds and burden-ridden people to printed pages that untie knots, loosen bonds, and free spirits that otherwise would have to remain in a vexation of unhappiness. If you are too busy or too far away from a library to visit it personally, why not write a note to the librarian, making it as specific as possible regarding your needs? The library staff can help you by mail.

3. Beware of Cure-All Literature

Some books offer a great deal of cure-all advice. Avoid them. The really great problems of life are not solved by magic, nor are the easy words of false prophets their answers. The true prophet knows that he "knows in part," and that he "prophesies in part." He reflects this humility about his own limitations in what he has to say to you. If a writer had *all* the answers to *all* of life's problems, there would be no need for prayer, because you would need to go no farther than to him. There would be no need for the church, because the help of a fellowship of weak and sinful people would be superfluous. There would be no need for God, for this person has put himself or herself in the place of God and is acting in a way that God in Christ never behaved. Therefore, avoid their panaceas and seek the literature written by those with a measure of caution and a desire to learn with you about your deep concerns.

4. Does the Author Lead You to Other Sources of Help?

Or does the author expect you to follow his or her advice without reference to anyone else? The dependable author will give you a clear idea of the other persons from whom he himself learned what he is giving you. He will undergird your confidence in other dependable sources of help, rather than expect you to rely upon his judgment alone. A helpful author never builds himself up at the expense of other people, but will "swear to his own hurt and not change" when it comes to reflecting to you the real value of the services of persons other than himself.

5. Does the Author Give You Some Humor, Encouragement, and Hope Along the Way?

Or are you beaten down with criticisms and negative attitudes that "take you apart" but do not help you to "put yourself back together again"? This kind of approach is particularly characteristic of some types of psychological literature. Many people who are suffering from nervous and emotional disorders read it as a sort of self-punishment procedure. They search avidly through technical literature for a set of terms with which to diagnose themselves. In reality the words have little value *to them* other than to be something by which they call themselves names. The best they come out with is a sort of "bootstraps" attempt to lift themselves out of their trouble by reading more and more books.

The useful book, however, is written with such humor and understanding as to impart both insight and support, criticism and encouragement, realism and hope. Cure-all literature gives a sort of optimism that is ungrounded and a confidence that is unreal. What you most need is the kind of book that goes to neither extreme but walks the narrow ridge between optimism and despair, namely, hope!

6. Is the Author a Recognized Authority on His Subject?

For instance, Evelyn M. Duvall, Sylvanus M. Duvall, David R. Mace, and Reuben Hill are nationally recognized as authorities on marriage and family difficulties. Leontine R. Young is an authority on the problems of the unwed mother, and Charles Stewart, on the problems of young people and the church. These persons are authorities for several reasons. For instance, they have had years of experience in dealing individually with the problems; they have done very careful research on the specific problems; and they have published on their subjects dependable literature that has been tested by use. One way of finding what a given author has published is to go to your library and ask to see the *Cumulative*

Book Index. Every book published by an author in English in a given month or year will be listed under the name of the author or cross-referenced under the name of the problem with which you are concerned. For example, "cerebral palsy" would be so listed as well as the names of the authors who write on such a subject.

7. Is the Book Publisher Reputable?

Another way of selecting a book is by the *publisher.* The book should be published by a reputable company, which follows sound business procedures. Consult a public-school teacher, a pastor, a doctor, a lawyer, or any professionally trained person, and he can help you to identify dependable and reputable publishers. A more immediate path would be through the storehouse of wisdom and knowledge of a good librarian. Some books are written by contract with a publisher who accepts the responsibility for manufacturing, publishing, and distributing the book. He pays the author a royalty. These are the more reliable publishers. Books published by "vanity presses," in which the author pays the publisher to produce his book, are often quite unreliable and misleading.

8. To Whom Was the Book Written?

A basic question to ask about any book desired for a specific need is, Was this book written to be read by the person who has the problem or need, or was it intended to be read by professional people, counselors who are engaged in the work of helping people? Many persons read heavy books on technical aspects of their problems instead of looking for easily read, plainly written, clearly understood books prepared for lay people who are in trouble. One of the major criticisms of the Kinsey reports is that they are too technical for the general reader. Most of the people who read them (or rather, most of the people who buy them) do not have the statistical and research ability to understand them. They would do much better to read an interpretation such as Seward Hiltner's *Sex Ethics and the Kinsey Reports* (Association Press, 1952) than to try to study the reports themselves. For the average lay person to read Kinsey's books with a view to getting help for personal sexual difficulties is like reading a book on surgery to get help for an inflamed appendix!

The audience, therefore, *to whom* a book is addressed is highly important. Pay attention to the preface of a book, noting the persons whom the author considers to be his audience.

9. Is the Book Brief and Clear?

Brevity and clarity are additional indications of the helpfulness of a book. A person who is deeply concerned with a specific life problem does not often in these busy days have time to search for help by delving into a long and complicated book. Someone will say under his breath, "But how about the Bible?" When faced without guidance with this entire large book, hundreds of pages in length, many readers often are unable to find the help that really is there. Actually the Bible is not *one* book, although it has a deep unity for those with eyes to see. It is a composite of many small books, each with different but related purposes, authors, audiences, and all concerned with man's relationship to God. Thus, for practical purposes, portions of the Bible sometimes are published separately, and from them many persons seem more easily to make precious sections their very own. Furthermore, the unusual popularity of small books of interpretation of portions of the Bible also shows that books are most helpful when they are brief and to the point.

10. What Are Other Reliable Sources?

Pamphlets and tracts are intended to meet specific needs. They do not stay in print very long, and new ones are always being released on a limited-printing basis. The best way to find dependable pamphlets and tracts for specific personal help is to write to reputable organizations for their annual list of publications. The following are a number of such organizations:

Alcoholics Anonymous, P.O. Box 1980, Grand Central Annex, New York, N.Y. 10017.

American Association of Retired Persons, 1225 Connecticut Avenue, N.W., Washington, D.C. 20036.

American Baptist Publication Society, Valley Forge, Pa. 19481.

American Institute of Family Relations, 5287 Sunset Boulevard, Los Angeles, Calif. 90027.

American Medical Association, 535 North Dearborn Street, Chicago, Ill. 60610.

American Social Health Association, 1740 Broadway, New York, N.Y. 10019.

Association for Family Living, 6 North Michigan Avenue, Chicago, Ill. 60602.

Auxiliary Council to the Association for the Advancement of Psychoanalysis, 329 East 62d Street, New York, N.Y. 10021.

Baptist Sunday School Board, Southern Baptist Convention, Tract Editor, 127 Ninth Avenue, North, Nashville, Tenn. 37208.

Child Study Association of America, 9 East 89th Street, New York, N.Y. 10028.

Child Welfare League of America, Inc. (adoption), 44 East 23d Street, New York, N.Y. 10010.

Concordia Publishing House, 3558 South Jefferson Street, St. Louis, Mo. 63118.

Division of Publication Documents, U.S. Government Printing Office, Washington, D.C. 20402.

Family Enrichment Bureau, 1615 Ludington Street, Escanaba, Mich. 49829.

Family Life Division, U.S. Catholic Conference, 1312 Massachusetts Avenue, N.W., Washington, D.C. 20005.

Family Life Publications, Inc., P.O. Box 427, Saluda, N.C. 28773.

Family Service Association of America, 44 East 23d Street, New York, N.Y. 10010.

Foster Parents Plan, Inc., 352 Park Avenue, South, New York, N.Y. 10010.

Health and Welfare Ministries, The United Methodist Church, 1200 Davis Evanston, Chicago, Ill. 60436.

Judean Society (divorce), 1075 Space Park Way No. 336, Mt. View, Calif. 94040.

La Leche League, (expectant and new mothers), 9696 Minneapolis Avenue, Franklin Park, Ill. 60131.

Maternity Center Association, 48 East 92d Street, New York, N.Y. 10028.

Methodist Publishing House, 201 Eighth Avenue, South, Nashville, Tenn. 37203.

National Association for Mental Health, Inc., 10 Columbus Circle, New York, N.Y. 10019.

National Association for Retarded Children, 2709 Avenue E, East, Arlington, Tex. 76011.

National Council of the Churches of Christ in the U.S.A., 475 Riverside Drive, New York, N.Y. 10027.

National Council on Alcoholism, 2 Park Avenue, New York, N.Y. 10016.

National Easter Seal Society for Crippled Children and Adults, 2023 West Ogden Avenue, Chicago, Ill. 60612.

National Rehabilitation Association, 1522 K Street, N.W., Washington, D.C. 20005.

Natural Family Planning Association, P.O. Box 250, New Haven, Conn. 06502.

Parents Without Partners Association, 80 Fifth Avenue, New York, N.Y. 10003.

Pastoral Psychology (magazine), 400 Community Drive, Manhasset, N.Y. 11030.

Planned Parenthood Federation of America, Inc., 810 Seventh Avenue, New York, N.Y. 10019.

Public Affairs Committee, 381 Park Avenue, South, New York, N.Y. 10016.

Science Research Associates, 259 East Erie, Chicago, Ill. 60611.

U.S. Department of Health, Education, and Welfare, 330 Independence Avenue, S.W., Washington, D.C. 20201.

The Westminster Press, Witherspoon Building, Philadelphia, Pa. 19107.

These lists can be effectively used in several ways by pastors, lay leaders, and counselors of every kind. Leaders themselves may order them and have a careful file of ready-reference material at hand. From time to time these lists should be reordered in order to have the most up-to-date publications. The person who has an intense need for help, about which he or she has not yet for several reasons found a counselor with whom to talk, can be helped partially by writing for these lists and ordering the titles that refer to particular problems. These materials can be ordered in quantity and placed in public literature racks in churches, schools, etc., in ways that will be appropriate. There can be a change box nearby into which payment for them can be placed. These lists may also be used to order materials for workshops, family-living institutes, and assembly conferences. Problems discussed in groups can be followed up with good materials for reading further about the issues involved. Finally, these materials can be handed by counselors to the individuals who have specific needs. Time saved in saying things that are said better in the pamphlets can be used to listen more intently to the individual's problem.

Part II

HELP ON SPECIAL PROBLEMS

3
Premarital Guidance

> Our heavenly Father, we thank thee that thou
> dost call men and women into a completing re-
> lationship of married love. Grant that the wisdom
> of the experienced and the taught may find its
> way to the inexperienced and uninstructed cou-
> ples through the channel of thy enduring truth.
> May all lovers' love increase in all manner of
> knowledge and spiritual perception through Jesus
> Christ our Lord. Amen.

Experienced marriage counselors regularly see people
whose homelife is like a garden grown up in weeds.
These thorny situations could have been prevented by
basic information, individual guidance, and spiritual fellowship if, as a *routine thing,* the couple had sought
help before they were married. *Every couple should
seek competent guidance before marriage.* Where can
they get such help?

A. RESOURCE PERSONS

The following persons or groups of persons are the
ones to whom you may turn for premarital guidance.

1. Your Pastor

Pastors are paying more and more attention to pre-marital guidance for young couples. Churches are becoming much more careful about the kind of persons whom their pastors unite in marriage, and pastors are expected to help couples prepare for marriage. Your pastor can give you instruction in the Christian faith if you are not both Christians. It is hoped that you will want your marriage to be a Christian covenant and vocation. If you are already a Christian, ask your pastor to help you understand the Christian teachings as they apply specifically to marriage. When a minister performs your wedding, you say to the community that you want your marriage to be Christian. Your pastor, furthermore, can give you guidance in the kind of wedding you would like to have. He has performed many weddings, but this will be your only one, in all probability. Therefore, draw on his experience here. Another thing your pastor can give you help on is how to have a distinctly Christian relationship in handling money and in becoming a good steward of all your finances, both in the way you earn and in the way you spend your money.

If there are vast religious differences between you and your partner, both of you should confer with your pastor, priest, or rabbi. Ask for the facts in their interpretation of these differences and for their personal observations. Reserve the right of decision until you have made your own prayers before God. Pastors, priests, and rabbis can minister to your parents' needs at the same time that they help you. If your parents are having difficulty in accepting the fact that you are grown now and are really going to get married, these counselors can act as ministers of reconciliation. In fact, your minister, priest, or rabbi *may* be the *only* professionally trained person who knows all the members of your family and has easy entry into their confidence.

If you are having problems with your parents, this should point you to the fact that in getting married you yourselves are moving toward becoming parents. What kind of parents will you be?

The experience of becoming parents yourselves also calls for great preparation and skill. Your pastor can lead you to basic and dependable sex information, information about planning your family, and information about child-rearing. He can key these things to the inspirations of the Christian faith.

In addition to all this, your pastor can function as a man of God with whom you can confess to God any sense of shame, guilt, or fear that may be holding you back from the fullest fellowship with God and with your mate in your forthcoming marriage. He can help you to discover the accepting forgiveness of God and the power to forgive others who may have trespassed against you. Finally, your pastor can lead you to the other persons in the community who can help you to prepare for marriage.

2. Your Doctor

You should seek out a doctor who has an adequate routine for examining and advising young couples before they are married. Some doctors will do only what the law requires, i.e., give a blood test and certify you for a license. But both the husband-to-be and the wife-to-be need a careful and complete physical examination. A thorough general practitioner can usually do for the husband what needs to be done. However, the bride should go to a gynecologist, for her examination will require specialized skill and insight. The gynecologist can advise her of the fitness of the sexual organs both for intercourse and for parenthood. Such a doctor can often suggest or perform minor therapies that will make both of these experiences more meaningful and successful.

One of the major reasons for consulting a physician is to establish a confident relationship as husband and wife to a family doctor. You promise to care for each other "in sickness and in health." When illness strikes, and it may be sooner than you think, you will both be prepared to care for each other if you already know a doctor you can call.

3. Your Financial Advisers

Different individuals turn to different kinds of persons for financial advice. A close business associate, an older fellow workman, a banker, an insurance person—all these and others perform this service. The groom particularly should pay attention to the problems of buying insurance. The names of newlyweds are listed in the newspapers, and insurance men put these names on their "prospect lists." You should be prepared ahead of time by conferring with a person whom you already know or with one who is dependably recommended to you. He can help you plan your life insurance, savings, investments, etc., in a way that will avoid overlapping, expensive, and useless programs. A good banker can help with any problems about borrowing, saving, and investing that you may have. This is particularly necessary if you expect to buy furniture, a house, or appliances, on credit-installment plans. Often a bank can solve your borrowing needs at a much less expensive rate than highly advertised retail outlets can. Objective, mature financial advisers can ordinarily coach you in such a way that you will not get head over heels in debt. They can give you authoritative insight as to how far a person with an income like yours can go in any direction without living beyond his means. If both of you do not carefully plan your finances, you may find yourself taking on two or three jobs to pay off your indebtedness, or your wife may need to work outside the home. You will have little time for each other. Then failures of understanding that bring grief may arise.

4. Agencies for Help

Your Family Service Organization, Marriage Counseling Center, or Planned Parenthood Clinic can be of assistance. Any one or more of the different agencies that are listed in Chapter 4 of this book can give you both direct and referral service on problems that arise. For instance, couples who are marrying a second time and have children by former marriages can go to one of these specialized service agencies for diagnostic and predictive help in facing the adjustments they must make. Couples who have severe conflicts during the engagement period over racial, cultural, and other kinds of differences can think through their problems at the clinic. If your pastors are having difficulty in being nonpartisan in an interfaith marriage situation, then agencies like this can often give you the objectivity that you need. If you are marrying a second time or even beyond the second time after having been divorced, you need to go to these agencies for skilled help that will enable you to discover your part in your previous marital failure. How can you learn from your previous unsuccessful attempt at marriage?

B. RESOURCES OF LITERATURE

Years ago approaches to premarital guidance amounted to little more than sneaking a book on sex to the couple. This is certainly a threadbare understanding of what marriage is all about. Your needs for literature include dependable books on the sexual aspects of marriage, but they certainly are much more extensive than that. Furthermore, books are useful, but they are not substitutes for secure personal understandings with your pastor, your doctor, your financial advisers, and others. The following books, therefore, are to be used along with the personal guidance you get—not as substitutes for it.

Certain books and pamphlets will give you an overview of the whole experience of marriage and family living. For example, Evelyn Millis Duvall, in the pamphlet *Building Your Marriage,* which has been published in the Public Affairs series (Pamphlet No. 113), gives a brief and helpful discussion of things you should be considering. You may be able to get this from your local Board of Health, Mental Health Commission, or Comprehensive Mental Health Center.

You will need some inspirational and spiritual interpretations of your adventure in marriage. William B. Ward's book *When You're Married* (John Knox Press, 1947) consists of fifteen devotionals for each of the first fifteen days of marriage, and makes excellent suggestions for the development of religious experience in the home. A more extensive devotional book, prepared especially for the couple who are to be married, is David R. Mace's book *Whom God Hath Joined* (The Westminster Press, 1953). This book is a necessity for every new home. Another volume by David Mace is *Success in Marriage* (Abingdon Press, 1958). Also helpful is Howard Hovde's book, *The Neo-Married* (Judson Press, 1968).

On the problem of finances, you can order from the Household Finance Corporation Money Management Institute, Prudential Plaza, Chicago, Ill. 60601, their *Money Management Library*. This was prepared by the Bureau of Business Research of Western Reserve University. It has materials on simplified budgeting, housing expenses, clothing expenses, children's spending, automobile- and appliance-buying, furniture-buying, etc. The pamphlets *Buyer, Be Wary!*, by Sidney Margolius, and *How to Stretch Your Money*, by the same author, can be obtained through Public Affairs Committee, 381 Park Avenue, South, New York, N.Y. 10016.

On the sexual and parental side of your life together, you and your mate will need some specific guidance. You can "square and plumb" your knowledge of sex by writing to Dr. Gelolo McHugh, Family Life Publications, Inc., P.O. Box 427, Saluda, N.C. 28773, asking him for the name and address of the nearest professional person who could give you the *Sex Knowledge Inventory*. Dr. McHugh devised this test in order to help people to complete their knowledge of the basic facts of sex and parenthood objectively. Likewise, you can order through Family Life Publications dependable literature fitted to your needs in the area of sex instruction for yourself now and for your children in the future.

On the side of emotional maturity and interpersonal competence, you will need to be certain of your understanding of your developmental history from a psychological point of view. As far as books will go in helping you with this, the following three will be most dependable:

Lewis J. Sherrill, *The Struggle of the Soul* (The Macmillan Company, 1951), gives a religious interpretation of the growth of personality in the light of the conception of faith set forth in the book of Hebrews in the New Testament.

George H. Preston, *The Substance of Mental Health* (Holt, Rinehart & Winston, Inc., 1946), is a happy, humorous, and factually trustworthy discussion of the way in which we are nurtured into a mentally healthy maturity. This book is brief, to the point, and simply written.

William Glasser, *Mental Health or Mental Illness? Psychiatry for Practical Action* (Perennial Library paperback, Harper & Row, Publishers, Inc., 1970), gives remarkably clear discussions of the typical adjustments of adults.

The latter two books, coupled with the theological interpretations of Lewis Sherrill, will present a rather well rounded, popularly written, but psychologically accurate picture of the development of your life together as man and wife.

See Alan F. Guttmacher's book, *Understanding Sex: A Young Person's Guide* (The New American Library, Inc., New York, N.Y. 10019). Also, Alan F. Guttmacher, *et al., The Complete Book of Birth Control* (Pocket Books, Inc., 630 Fifth Avenue, New York, N.Y. 10011), is very helpful on this important concern.

The American Medical Association (535 North Dearborn Street, Chicago, Ill. 60610) publishes three excellent pamphlets on sex education: *Facts Aren't Enough, Contraceptive Drugs and Devices,* and *Infertility.*

Some fine volumes on the process of pregnancy and childbirth, as well as parenthood as a lifework, are: *Husbands and Pregnancy: A Handbook for Expectant Fathers,* by William Genne; Eve S. Featheringill's *How to Be a Successful Mother* for the wife and mother; and for the young couple who are marrying with the girl already pregnant, Charles Tooman's *And They Said We Had to Get Married.* All three of these frank, clear, and helpful books are published by the Abbey Press at St. Meinrad, Ind. 47577.

C. INTERFAITH MARRIAGE

One thing more needs to be said about premarital guidance: many marriages today are being effected across the lines of the great faiths. Since Vatican II, a more varied picture of Catholic and Protestant marriages has begun to develop. Probably the most common interfaith marriage in this country is between members of the Protestant and Roman Catholic faiths. If you are contemplating an interfaith marriage, it is very important that you take several steps. First, you should get all the facts that you can about both faiths, especially the specific demands that are made of you as to your religious practice and the rearing of your children. Each of you should consult your pastor, priest, or rabbi. If you do not have such a person, you should go to a faculty member of the department of religion of your denominational college or to a faculty member of a theological seminary. These persons can give you factual information. Also, read an older book by James A. Pike, *If You Marry Outside Your Faith* (Harper & Brothers, 1954), now in paperback, in which you will find carefully gathered research materials of each of the major religious groups on marriage relationships. The book gives straight, factually grounded guidance for couples of differing faiths.

Secondly, you should seek the objective help of an experienced counselor. Many times your wanting to marry a person far out of the range of your traditional religion may be mixed with motives that need clarification. For example, a very common motive is a half-conscious effort to hurt someone who would disapprove of the marriage. The reasons for wanting to hurt a parent could have existed before the possibility of the marriage. If your pastor, priest, or rabbi is flexible (although not wishy-washy) enough to respect your integrity without at the same time hiding the realistic facts from you, then you are very fortunate. But by all means seek the help of a competent marriage counselor (who, it can be hoped, *is* your pastor) in this situation and think the matter through thoroughly. The unforeseen complications, for instance, that can follow the expectations of the Roman Catholic Church are many. The Roman Catholic member of an interfaith marriage is required to make a pledge to rear the children of the forthcoming marriage according to the Roman Catholic faith.

That promise is as follows:

> I reaffirm my faith in Jesus Christ and, with God's help, intend to continue living that faith in the Catholic Church.

I promise to do all in my power to share the faith
I have received with our children by having them
baptized and reared as Catholics.

Then, so says the document approved by the National
Conference of Catholic Bishops of the United States,
November 16, 1970, effective January 1, 1971:

At an opportune time before marriage, and preferably as a part of the usual pre-marital instructions, the non-Catholic must be informed of
the promises and responsibility of the Catholic. No
precise manner or occasion of informing the non-
Catholic is prescribed. It may be done by the
priest, deacon or the Catholic party. *No formal
statement of the non-Catholic is required.* [Italics
ours.] But the mutual understanding of this question [*sic*] beforehand should prevent possible disharmony that might otherwise arise during married life. (Taken from "Guidelines for Mixed
Marriages," *The Catholic Mind,* Vol. LXIX, No.
1250 [Feb., 1971], pp. 47–55.)

The guidelines say that two separate religious services
for the Catholics and the non-Catholics are not permitted, but that "with the permission of the local Or-
dinary and the consent of the appropriate authority of
the other church, a non-Catholic minister may be invited
to participate in the Catholic marriage service by giving
additional prayers, blessings, words of greeting or ex-
hortation. If the marriage is not a part of the Eucharist
celebration the minister may also be invited to read a
lesson, and/or preach." (Cf. *Ecumenical Directory,* Part
I, p. 56.)

The document does not mention the problem of birth
control, which is very important for the Catholic and

non-Catholic to consider. The only method of birth control sanctioned by the Catholic Church at this writing is
the rhythm method of abstaining from sexual intercourse
during the period of fertility in the woman's menstrual
cycle. These times occur during the week preceding the
menstrual flow, and during the period of about twelve
weeks after the birth of a child. The use of "the pill,"
foam, a diaphragm, condom, or an intrauterine device is
not approved by the Catholic Church. This factor should
be thoroughly discussed and a frank commitment to each
other made prior to marriage. A mutual understanding of
birth-control measures beforehand also is necessary in
the event that "possible disharmony that might arise
during married life" will not be further complicated by
this matter.

Lest we overconcentrate on the Catholic-Protestant
marriage, let us hasten to say that real stresses over religious differences can grow up between people of the
same religious grouping, and between people who are
of different Protestant persuasions. Some people are ob-
serving that the most intense religious conflicts of the
1970's seem to be appearing within denominations rather
than between them. Thus persons marrying should be
knowledgeable about their own and other denominations. Frank S. Mead's *A Handbook of Denominations in
the United States,* 5th ed. (Abingdon Press), is a reliable
storehouse of information.

4
Marriage Conflict

> Increase the wisdom, skill, and number of those,
> our Father, who lay to heart the ministry of recon-
> ciliation between members of families. Help
> them to discover the foundations thou hast laid
> in creation and redemption whereby men and
> women come to dwell in such accord as to glorify
> thee, through Jesus Christ our Lord. Amen.

When you need financial help, you are not reluctant
to seek outside assistance if you can find someone who
is willing to serve you. You are willing even to pay interest on money for such help. When you need medical
help, especially if you are in great pain, you are even
eager to get a doctor to relieve your distress through
his specialized knowledge and skill. In the same way,
when you and members of your family get to the point
that you can no longer work out constructive solutions
to problems that emerge in your developing family life,
you should seek outside help. To do so is a form of ex-
pressing your own love for the other person, not a be-
trayal of him or her. If it is at all possible, the partner
should agree with you to seek help. In most instances,
the partner should know that you are seeking outside
help, lest he or she feel betrayed by your secrecy. Also,

the person seeking to help you is able to feel more secure in that most counselors would want to know if their own spouses were conferring with other people.

When communication fails, you may be tempted to go on a silence strike, a "pouting spree," to threaten divorce, or even to pack up and leave. You may even be tempted to talk to some person of the opposite sex who appears for the moment more attractive than your husband or wife. Naturally, all these approaches may complicate rather than relieve your distressing situation. Therefore, you really need a trained and dedicated person of one of the helping professions with whom to confer. You need help, and the following are persons and resources upon whom you can draw.

Before you seek another person's help, you probably will start looking for literature on family problems. Howard J. and Charlotte H. Clinebell's *The Intimate Marriage* (Harper & Row, Publishers, Inc., 1970) is a good place to start. Gibson Winter, *Love and Conflict* (Dolphin Book, Doubleday & Company, Inc. n.d.), and George R. Bach and Peter Wyden, *The Intimate Enemy*, paperback, are also reliable guides.

Your *pastor* spends much of his time in marriage and family counseling. Increasing numbers of pastors have had specific training in this area of service. If you do not have a pastor, a call to the denomination of your choice, to the local Council of Churches office, or to the pastor of a trusted friend will help to establish such a relationship. Your pastor not only will be able to help you himself, but he will know other people in the community to help you with specific problems. Expect to confer with your pastor more than once. Ask him to study the problem and let you return to talk it over with him after he has time to think about it.

Many churches and groups of churches are adding specially trained persons to their staff to help with these problems. A few churches are providing marriage clinic services in association with their family-life education programs. Groups of churches such as the Protestant Church Council in Richmond, Virginia, for instance, provide skilled counseling for disturbed and unhappy families.

Your *Family Service Organization,* usually listed by this name in your telephone book, offers extensive and intensive types of marriage counseling. Conflicts between husbands and wives, parents and children, parents and older persons such as their own parents in the home, and the like, are of real concern to the personnel of the Family Service Organizations. Trained social workers give very careful diagnosis and treatment of the marriage difficulty on a social casework basis. If psychiatric or psychoanalytic service is indicated, consultant members of the staff of the organization are available. These organizations on the local scene are members of the Family Service Association of America. A listing of them and their addresses, entitled *Directory of Member Agencies of the Family Service Association of America,* can be ordered from the Family Service Association of America, 44 East 23d Street, New York, N.Y. 10010. A pastor does well to have one of these at hand for advising his church members when they go into other territories.

Let us suggest the following *national organizations.* They provide various types of guidance to counseling services and literature that will meet needs for marriage and family life:

American Association of Marriage Counselors, 149–157 Willetts Point Boulevard, New York, N.Y. 10000. Has information about marriage counselors and marriage-counseling services throughout the United States.

American Social Health Association, Inc., 1740 Broadway, New York, N.Y. 10019. Member agencies in many states.

Family Service Association of America, 44 East 23d Street, New York, N.Y. 10010. Has member agencies in cities over the country which offer casework services.

National Association for Mental Health, 10 Columbus Circle, New York, N.Y. 10019. Roster of mental hygiene and child-guidance clinics available.

National Council on Family Relations, 1219 University Avenue, S.E., Minneapolis, Minn. 55414. National membership of professional persons from related fields in the United States, Canada, and several foreign countries.

Planned Parenthood Federation of America, 810 Seventh Avenue, New York, N.Y. 10019.

A letter to any of these central offices will get a response telling you of qualified persons in your area to help you. Also, they can provide you with a directory of these centers for a small fee, sometimes without cost.

Specific *religious organizations* representing the various branches of the Judeo-Christian heritage have been developed for the strengthening of the moral and spiritual foundations of the home. They can give guidance in helpful literature and point toward specific counseling agencies for special needs.

Roman Catholic
Family Life Division, United States Catholic Conference, 1312 Massachusetts Avenue, N.W., Washington, D.C. 20005.

Jewish

Rabbinical Assembly of America, 3080 Broadway, New York, N.Y. 10027.

Protestant

Joint Department of Family Life, National Council of the Churches of Christ in the U.S.A., 475 Riverside Drive, New York, N.Y. 10027.

Since the first publication of this book, pastoral counseling centers have been established all over the United States. They are staffed by persons who are active, approved members, fellows, or diplomates and have demonstrated their competence as pastoral counselors. The administrative secretary, Office of the American Association of Pastoral Counselors, 31 West 10th Street, New York, N.Y. 10011, Tel. (212) 260-4170, can supply a list of agencies and counselors and answer further inquiries.

5

Sexual Difficulties

> Eternal God, who hast created us in thine own image, and in whose will is our peace, we thank thee for thy truth which makes us free and for thy love which never disappears. Forgive us our trespasses as we forgive those who trespass against us. Give us faith in the power of thy grace to renew, establish, and strengthen those who have wandered from Christ's way of life. Help those who have lost their way in their sex behavior to remember and to obey the words of Jesus: "Neither do I condemn you; go, and do not sin again." Amen.   (*O. T. Binkley.*)

Many people live out their lives in quiet desperation because of stresses and strains that they consciously feel to be sexual problems. They long to find dependable literature, for much that is written on this subject is not to be trusted. They long to find counselors, informed and capable of patient forgiveness, with whom they can safely talk and by whom they will be taken seriously.

Sexual difficulties are of differing levels of seriousness and appear at different stages of personal maturity in the psychosexual development of a person. The following groups of persons represent those who most often need help:

1. *Parents Who Are Nonplussed or Threatened by Their Children's Questions About Sex*

The parents themselves need dependable, scientifically accurate information. Two excellent ways for getting this are available. One is to read the books by the American Medical Association, entitled *Facts Aren't Enough* and *The Miracle of Life* (535 North Dearborn Street, Chicago, Ill. 60610).

The other way is to order the *Sex Knowledge Inventory* through your pastor from Family Life Publications, Inc., P.O. Box 427, Saluda, N.C. 28773. This agency can also answer individual requests for reading materials on various problems. The American Social Health Association, Inc., 1740 Broadway, New York, N.Y. 10019, has published a pamphlet entitled *A Formula for Sex Education,* which gives a graduated program of sex education for growing children. The American Medical Association, 535 North Dearborn Street, Chicago, Ill. 60610, has a series of pamphlets on sex education for different age groups: *Sex Education for the Preschool Child,* by Harold E. Jones and Katherine Read; *Sex Education for the 10-Year-Old,* by Marjorie Bolles; *Sex Education for the Adolescent Boy and Girl,* by George Corner and Carney Landis; *Sex Education for the Married Couple,* by Emily Hartshorne Mudd; *Sex Education for the Woman at Menopause,* by Carl G. Hartman. The Child Study Association of America, 9 East 89th Street, New York, N.Y. 10028, has a pamphlet that has been in use for a long time entitled *When Children Ask About Sex.*

A new breakthrough in the understanding of sex has been brought about by William H. Masters and Virginia E. Johnson. A layman's report on their research has been edited by Ruth and Edward Brecher, entitled *An Analysis of Human Sexual Response* (The New American Library, Inc., 1966). This is a popular paperback volume and can be bought in many department stores and drugstores as well as in bookstores.

Accurate information about sex, rightly timed, is a very important need. Books can furnish that. But relaxed, guilt-free attitudes, with a spiritually mature enjoyment of sexual happiness on the part of the parents, are far more important than factual data. The tonal communication is more important than the verbal communication! The use of animals as examples of sex behavior is not an inspiring way of approaching sex information for children. The child may have fears of animals, because city children have increasingly less access to a happy relationship to the animal world. It is better to use the relationship of the family itself, when the occasion arises for "teachable moments," to impart sex information.

You may need to talk with a good family counselor, such as those listed in Chapter 4 of this book, if you continue to have stress in your relationship to your children concerning their sex behavior and attitudes.

2. *Persons Who Are Troubled About Masturbation Need Sympathetic Understanding and Mature Encouragement*

Old superstitions—that masturbation is likely to cause a person to become insane; that handling one's sex organs renders one incapable of marriage relationships; that masturbation causes one to have skin disorders, etc. —need to be exposed for what they are. All of them are just not so. If, therefore, the sense of shame over this problem continues to bother you, the thing you should do is seek out a trained counselor who can interpret it for you and help you to clear up your feelings about it. Lists of these counselors are found in Chapter 4.

3. *Married Persons Who Suffer from Frigidity or Impotence*

Those persons need help who for any reason feel that they are incapable of full sexual satisfaction. Although they continue to bear their burden of unhappiness and to be a problem to their partners, happiness is often waiting for persons like this. Their problem can safely be discussed with a mature and well-trained pastor. Pastors with clinical pastoral training have been informed as to how to deal with this kind of difficulty and they can suggest other counselors able to help resolve deeper causes of frigidity and impotence. The Masters and Johnson research has revolutionized much of contemporary thinking on this subject. These studies are in a large, technical volume which takes considerable professional know-how to decipher. However, the authors have approved a popular paperback study "written clearly and in nontechnical language." This summary and interpretation of their research is entitled *Understanding Human Sexual Inadequacy,* by Fred Belliveau and Lin Richter (Bantam Books, Inc., 1970.)

4. *Persons with Homosexual Problems*

Persons who fear homosexuality to a hindering extent, persons who have actually become involved in isolated homosexual activity, and persons who have adopted homosexuality as a chosen way of life need the help of both intelligent reading and skilled counseling for their problems. The three groups of people we have named above present distinctly different kinds of problems, although they tend to classify themselves in the same category. They lump themselves together out of ignorance and fear. The word "homosexual" should be applied only to that person who has persistently and intentionally sustained a habitual pattern of sexual relationships with a member of the same sex. Other types of behavior are better described in terms such as "confused sexual identity" or "occasional homosexual activity." Such a strong taboo prevails in American culture against tenderness and gentleness in men and strength and aggressiveness in women that the end result is a *fear of homosexuality* which is much more prevalent than the actions and patterns themselves. Parents who are concerned about sons or daughters becoming involved homosexually can find help and encouragement by reading *Growing Up Straight,* by Peter and Barbara Wyden (Stein & Day, 1968). An authoritative scientific statement of the whole problem and therapeutic help for persons needing it is to be found in the article *Report on Homosexuality* by the Group for the Advancement of Psychiatry (419 Park Avenue, South, New York, N.Y. 10016). It is best to order this report through some professional person, such as your doctor or minister.

A penetrating theological analysis of the problem has been presented in the book by Irving Bieber, *et al., Homosexuality* (A Vintage Book, Random House, Inc., n.d.), and it is discussed briefly in the book by Wayne E. Oates, *The Bible in Pastoral Care* (The Westminster Press, 1953). One of the more recent studies is H. Kimball Jones, *Toward a Christian Understanding of the Homosexual* (Association Press, 1966).

As for counseling, the most immediate help available

to those who suffer with this problem or with the fear of it is from the pastoral and marriage counseling agencies listed in Chapter 4. The experienced guidance counselor in colleges and universities often has clinical insight for dealing with the person who merely has the fear of homosexuality and is working out his concept of himself as a sexual person. However, the person who has a long-term, ingrained, and overt pattern of persistently preferred homosexual behavior needs highly specialized therapeutic help. This help can be found in several ways.

Pastors who have also had thorough clinical training, have been taught how best to help you or can be of continuing aid. This implies long-term counseling help, for the problem is a personality disorder, although considerable public activism on the part of confirmed homosexuals is making a bid for homosexuality as a bona fide life-style in a time of moral pluralism. Furthermore, members of the American Association of Marriage Counselors, whose central office is at 149–157 Willetts Point Boulevard, New York, N.Y. 10000, are competent resource persons.

Clinical psychiatrists occasionally can be of real service to the confirmed homosexual. Usually they prefer to work with persons who are psychotic. Many do not consider homosexuality to be the kind of problem to which they can give their time most rewardingly, but the exceptions to this are numerous. The psychiatrist who can maintain patience with these persons and who also has had some intensive training in psychoanalytic orientation is most helpful. Many psychiatrists, furthermore, who have *not* had psychoanalytic training nevertheless have a tremendous capacity to accept people regardless of their particular symptoms. These doctors can often by sheer dedication and wisdom drawn from long-suffering patience in dealing with people help the homosexual to develop a more normal way of life—to arrest the symptoms, as it were.

At the time of the first edition of this book, psychoanalysts seemed to have had more success than others in the treatment of overt homosexuality. However, since then considerable study has been done on homosexual behavior. Much of this behavior is pseudohomosexuality or symptomatic behavior. See Lionel Ovesey, *Homosexuality and Pseudohomosexuality* (Science House, Inc., 1969). The reality therapists such as William Glasser and transactional therapists such as Eric Berne have approached this as well as a wide variety of other problems as a basic failure in personal responsibility or a moral lapse. They are exercising a helpful corrective in psychiatry. Older psychiatric treatment is extensive and takes much time. It is intensive and plumbs the depths of the total organization of personality. It is expensive and involves the commitment of great quantities of time by one person who has spent most of his life in getting the education and highly specialized training to do the work that needs to be done. Before a person undergoes such therapy he should read the book edited by Karen Horney entitled *Are You Considering Psychoanalysis?* (Norton Library paperback, W. W. Norton & Company, Inc., 1946). This internationally recognized psychoanalyst, along with several other analysts, discusses in detail the issues at stake in psychoanalytic treatment. Addresses of the various related institutes are found at the end of Chapter 14.

Regardless of whom you go to for help in any kind of sexual difficulty, bear in mind that the attendant sense

of guilt and burden of need for forgiveness in your relationship to God is always of concern to your pastor.
He can sustain you with a sense of trust and hope as you
deal with the barriers to effective prayer, the feelings of
isolation and loneliness, and the need for an everyday
friend who can be trusted. Think of him as a fellow pilgrim with you as you move out of the immaturity of an
irresponsible way of being sexual into the mature sense
of faith that characterizes the person who takes full responsibility in marriage for an effective and creative
sexual life.

6
Birth Control

Our heavenly Father, we thank thee for thy fore-
seeing providence, that thou didst love us in
Christ from the foundations of the world. May
we share in thy planning for our lives by sharing
in thy foresight for the children thou wilt give
us. Purify our hearts of irresponsibility and self-
love, even when it poses as obedience to thy
laws. Help us to bring the discoveries of science
under the dominion of thy sovereign grace. For
thou hast not made anything common or un-
clean. All things are for thy glory. Amen.

Many couples do not wish to have children immediately after marriage and want to determine the time of
the arrival of their children. Others, for many reasons,
desire not to have any more children. The basic ethical
problem here, it seems, is that the decision whether or
not to have children at all or not to *want* children at all
is opened up in a way today that has not been apparent
before in history. The availability of "the pill," the lib-
eralization of abortion laws, and the extreme tentative-
ness with which people enter marriage have placed the
ethical certainties of the past in jeopardy. There is no
absolute control of human fertility except total absti-

nence from sexual intercourse or sterilization. The possibility of having children is implicit in the vows of marriage, from both a theological and an interpersonal point of view. But this ethical decisiveness gets all mixed up in people's minds with other issues. One of these is the spacing of children. The other is limiting the size of the family, i.e., the number of children. The spacing and the limitation of the number of children is usually for economic, social, and interpersonal reasons. It can be for profoundly religious and ethical reasons when it involves the health of the mother, the overworking of the father to support too many children, and the exploitation of the family by churches who consider the decisions about the family to be the prerogative of the church and not of the husband and wife.

You have, therefore, need for something more than superficial help on this particular problem. You need to think through the deepest implications of it. The book by Joseph Fletcher, *Morals and Medicine* (Princeton University Press, 1954; paperback, Beacon Press, Inc., 1960), will be unusually helpful. He calls this "our right to control parenthood." He looks upon parenthood as a voluntary, and not a fatalistic, vocation. You have a right to choose within certain limits. He looks upon parenthood as made for man, and not man for parenthood.

Through the Planned Parenthood Federation of America, Inc., you can get several pamphlets that will help you with both the moral and religious aspects of birth control and with the specific ways of controlling birth. Titles of these materials are available in their publications list, which can be received free by writing to them at 810 Seventh Avenue, New York, N.Y. 10019. Also, the American Medical Association, 535 North Dearborn

Street, Chicago, Ill. 60610, has a pamphlet entitled *Contraceptive Drugs and Devices* which you should have.

If you fall into any of the following groups, you may need to seek birth-control guidance:

1. *Brides and Grooms*

Premarital guidance on sexual fitness for marriage is a primary necessity. A thorough premarital physical examination, consisting of more than just a blood test to indicate freedom from venereal disease, is always advisable. Many of the difficulties of parenthood and sexual behavior, especially those arising from the fear of pregnancy or of possible causes of sterility, can be detected early through a careful medical examination. Both the bride and groom need these examinations. Birth-control advice can be obtained from your physician at this time.

2. *Persons Suffering from Frigidity or Impotence*

Those who are unable to participate either partially or completely in marital relations, a quite prevalent problem, need help in addition to birth-control guidance. A planned parenthood clinic, however, can refer you to that help. Several pamphlets on this problem are available through the American Institute of Family Relations, 5287 Sunset Boulevard, Los Angeles, Calif. 90027.

The fear of pregnancy is occasionally a major factor in hindering husbands and wives from full companionship and response in sexual relations. Faulty techniques of birth control, such as interruption of sexual intercourse through withdrawal before the man reaches a climax, can cause much irritability, moodiness, and unhappiness in the daily life of husband and wife.

3. *Those Who Do Not Want More Children*

The inalienable right of every child is to be wanted.

For many reasons, you may not want more children than you already have. For instance, the health of the mother, the fact that you are in a kind of work that requires your family to travel a great deal of the time, the fact that your economic and housing situations are already over-taxed, or the fact that the stability of your marriage requires that the wife be freed for closer association with the husband in his work, etc., may prevail to make more children inadvisable.

4. *Those Who Want to Space Their Children*

Many people, simply in keeping with necessity and psychological wisdom, want to plan the arrivals of their children. Let us suggest dependable sources for such guidance.

Your *minister* will know sources of information about the problems of birth control. You may need expert guidance and education. His training will make him especially helpful in discussing the theological and ethical questions that you may raise concerning birth control. The very fact that you may be a bit timid about talking with him may reflect a sense of guilt about the whole matter. But spiritual guidance is certainly needed here. Keep looking until you find it in the pastoral leadership of your community. If your local hospitals have clinically trained chaplains, you will be more certain to get help there.

Your *general physician* can give you advice of a general nature on birth-control problems. His information will also enable him to give you specific advice, particularly about the more permanent types of birth control such as the tying off of the Fallopian tubes in the mother or the irreversible type of vasectomy in the father. The accompanying sense of uneasiness may need the attention of a marriage counselor such as those listed in Chapter 4 of this book.

The mother should, if at all possible, seek the specific advice of a *gynecologist*. Such a doctor is, as has been said earlier, an expert in the problems of feminine hygiene, medical diagnosis and therapy, and maternal health. A gynecologist can give the wife and husband the kind of specialized supervision in the processes of parenthood and birth control that they need. The husband should not let an overanxious feeling about the expense keep him from taking his wife to such a doctor, because often the expense is no more than that of a general practitioner's services. Many persons of modest incomes may suppose that going to a gynecologist for the care of the wife or to a pediatrician for the care of the child is something that only people who are a little "uppity," "highbrow," or who "have money" or "pull" do. But skilled laborers today in many instances make more money than white-collar workers, and they should never let some imaginary difference between them and their neighbors prevent them from getting the best help available. The dirt on the hands of a worker does not decide what his dollar will buy. So, even if you have only modest means, look for the best. It will often cost you less!

For routine, inexpensive, and carefully organized clinic help on birth-control instruction, such as a prescription for oral contraceptives, the fitting of diaphragms, the prescription of a foam, an intrauterine device, or the teaching of the rhythm method of birth control, you should go to the nearest Planned Parenthood Clinic. Through much criticism, real suffering, and courage that arises to the level of heroism, the professional people associated with these clinics have made help available to you at great cost to themselves and little cost to you. Often the doctors in these clinics are the same doctors who minister in their private offices to the wealthiest people in the community. You get the best the community can offer in these clinics. You can consult your local telephone directory for the "Planned Parenthood Clinic." If it is not listed, write directly to the Planned Parenthood Federation of America, Inc. The address of the national office is 810 Seventh Avenue, New York, N.Y. 10019. They will supply you with the exact address of the clinic nearest you. Pastors, doctors, lawyers, and others will do well to order a copy of their *Directory of Clinic Service: Birth Control and Infertility*.

5. *Those Who Are "Starstruck"*

Often adolescent young persons will refuse to use birth-control measures, even though they are planning to have sexual intercourse. Their reason—if we may misuse the word—is that to plan intercourse is unromantic and birth control calls for planning. How naïve!

ABORTION AS A FINAL ATTEMPT AT BIRTH CONTROL

Considerable attention is given to abortion in the public press today. Increasing numbers of localities such as Hawaii and New York have legalized abortions, and before this book is in print there probably will be others. Crusaders have established "abortion counseling" services. The authors of this book take the position that to become "single issue" counselors on such things as abortion and the draft, important as these issues are, is not the most desirable kind of counseling. Our reasons are that counseling easily becomes propaganda instead of an examination of the wider range of other alternatives, because it takes into consideration only *one* facet of a person's life without regard for the totality of the person's needs, and because it is often done by persons who have not disciplined themselves in any depth understanding of personality and in the "drudgery" of most routine and less dramatic kinds of counseling.

However, abortion when done by a medical doctor who has the legal freedom to do so *is* an option that should be considered as one of the alternatives in such instances as the following:

a. A pregnancy in an exceptionally young girl, such as a twelve- to sixteen-year-old.

b. A pregnancy where medical examination reveals that the child will be severely retarded and/or malformed.

c. A pregnancy in a married woman by a person not her husband or in a widow or divorcee who is the sole support of other children.

d. A pregnancy in which a previous history of mental illness and the possibility that another episode will be precipitated by the birth of the child, especially when the mother is suicidal.

e. A pregnancy that was the result of incestuous sexual behavior.

f. A pregnancy that was the result of rape or even partial consent.

g. A pregnancy in a mother who is mentally retarded to such an extent that she is not responsible for her behavior or for the care of the child.

In the final analysis, in most cases only the mother herself can really make this decision, but we write down these concrete situations as guidelines for thinking about abortion as a "last resort" kind of birth control, as the result of failures to use or failures of the efficiency of other methods of birth control, as an ethical dilemma that calls for the closest of attention by medical doctors and pastors. At best, abortion is a compromise between the lesser of two sad situations, and a "second chance" ethic is needed to justify it.

Beyond the present preoccupation with abortion is the future possibility of new breakthroughs in birth control. Perhaps new means of birth control for which men are primarily responsible will be discovered. At present only the vasectomy, or total sterilization of the man, and the condom prophylactic are distinctly available to men. Furthermore, recent news indicates that medical researchers report promises of longer-term oral contraceptives which do not have troublesome side effects. But it will be at least 1973 or 1974 before these can be distributed to the public, according to a report by Andrew V. Schally, of Tulane Medical Center, at the Endocrine Society meeting in San Francisco on June 25, 1971.

7

Sterility

O Thou who dost smile with approval upon our desire for children, save us all from the idolatry of that desire. Grant these thy servants the sense of peace and serenity that comes from surrender of every defective motive for wanting children. Bring into focus the powers of thy mysterious creativity and the goodwill of a loving and wise community to meet the real needs of the husband and wife who pour out their complaints of their childlessness to thee. Amen.

Hannah poured out her complaint before God. She wanted children and could not have them. Not even the tender love of Elkanah could help her. What can be done today for those mothers and fathers who are unable to have children, who are sterile?

Sterility is not always the "fault" of the woman. Both men and women share in the causation of this difficulty. Therefore, as in other problems affecting the whole of life, careful clinical diagnosis first by your general physician and then by a sterility specialist is highly indicated. Both the husband and the wife will need a thorough medical examination. The couple should be careful not to confuse *sterility*, which means the lack of ability (for any of various reasons) to produce a fertilized ovum to begin conception, with *impotence,* which is a lack of desire or ability to have adequate sex relations. Psychologically, the two may be related, but they are not the same. Therefore, the couple should go as a couple to their general physician for a complete study of the problem and seek referral to a specialist in sterility problems. "Doctors nowadays have many elaborate tests for determining the underlying causes of sterility, but they are paying considerable attention to the patient's *general* health." (Joseph D. Wassersug, *More Help for Childless Couples* [American Medical Association, 535 North Dearborn Street, Chicago, Ill. 60610]; reprinted from *Hygeia,* Nov. and Dec., 1947.) But real caution should be exerted here. General practitioners in the main are not fully trained in sterility guidance, diagnosis, and therapy to handle the problem alone. Specialized help should be sought. Couples have been told by their general practitioner that they could not have children. They went for another medical opinion from a specialist in sterility and after some careful treatment were able to have a child. One of the most useful books a couple can read is by William T. Bassett, *Counseling the Childless Couple* (Fortress Press, 1969).

One inexpensive procedure for getting sterility tests and advisory help is through the Planned Parenthood Federation of America. Here it is done on a "package deal" basis and the cost is scaled according to the income of the family. The national office will respond to your individual request for the name of the director and the address of the nearest Planned Parenthood Clinic. A quicker way is to look in your telephone directory under Planned Parenthood Federation of America, Inc. The national office is at 810 Seventh Avenue, New York, N.Y. 10019.

Bear in mind that the problem of sterility has some profound psychological and spiritual overtones. You may be so tensely drawn over this problem that it will cause you to overlook the other less obvious frustrations you are suffering. As a result your other problems will go unconsidered. They will further complicate your chances to be the secure person who can wisely care for a child *at this time*. Therefore, you may need skillful counseling from a clinically trained pastor who understands both the psychological and the religious issues at stake. He will, if he deems it advisable, help you to find other counselors who may be indicated to serve you at this point. This does not mean that you are getting ready to "flip your lid" or "lose your mind," but it does mean that you can become so tense over this particular helplessness that you will get in your own way.

The important thing to do in the face of this kind of helplessness is to get the best medical advice and spiritual help you can find. Do not overlook the fact that intelligent, realistic, and spiritually mature prayer avails much in coping with this great need. Seek the guidance of your pastor in how to pray. We do not many times know how to pray as we ought, and need to turn to some shepherd, just as the disciples turned to Jesus to be taught to pray. This is the great function of Christian pastors.

In addition, you will want to read something on this subject to prepare your attitudes for the best reception of the help that is available to you. The first place you should turn to is the Bible, because this problem is prominent in the thinking of the people of both the Old

and the New Testament. Read the following passages:
Gen. 17:9–21; 21:1–7; I Sam. 1:1 to 2:11; Luke 1:5–80;
Heb. 11:8–12. Then, too, in order that you may be specifically informed about the moral implications of some
of the most recent discoveries in the treatment of sterility, you should read Joseph Fletcher's book *Morals and
Medicine,* especially his chapter on the use of artificial
insemination, which he subtitles "Our Right to Overcome Childlessness."

From the medical side of the problem, some good articles have been written, which are available to you at a
few cents' cost through the Planned Parenthood Federation of America, at the above-mentioned address. One
is their current listing entitled *To Those Denied a Child.*
Another article, by Joseph D. Wassersug, previously
quoted in this chapter, may be ordered from the American Medical Association, *More Help for Childless Couples.*

8

Unwanted Pregnancy

> O God, who hast required each of us to act justly, to love loyalty, and to walk wisely before thee, we are grateful that thou dost hear and receive honest expressions of disappointment and confusion. Grant to this woman the grace and wisdom to search after thee in regard to her pregnancy. Our heavenly Father, thou hast in Jesus Christ our Lord urged all little children to come unto thee. We pray that if this woman is to become a mother, thy love will enable her to see her child's need for its own sake alone. In her rebellion against the domination of others, may she find true freedom in responsibility to thee for her decision. Amen.

Nathaniel Hawthorne in his priceless novel *The Scarlet Letter* tells the story of Hester Prynne, an unfortunate girl who became the mother of a child out of wedlock, and her secret lover, the minister of the church. Hawthorne carefully draws a picture of the frailties of the whole community that lay beneath this event, without at the same time ignoring the necessity for an adult kind of responsibility on Hester's part. He also expresses the depth of the despair of the father of the child. This particularly poignant, embarrassing, and threatening experience is no respecter of persons. It happens among the privileged and the underprivileged, the pious and the not-so-pious, the respectable and the unrespectable. It is another "leveler" of the little legalistic distinctions that people use to insist upon being different from one another. God has used such experiences *after they happened* to bring whole families and communities into an awareness of their need of his love and understanding help.

If you—or any of your loved ones or friends—therefore fall into this difficult situation of having an unwanted pregnancy, bear in mind that real understanding, forgiveness, and help are available. The couple who think the woman is pregnant will be tempted to do several things that they should *never* do. To the contrary, they should *always* do certain other things that they may be too upset to think of doing. What are these things?

Things they should never do. The woman may be tempted to destroy herself, thinking that this is the end of her world. This is the end of a certain part of her life, that part in which her potential for motherhood is a secret to the universe about her. The couple, married or unmarried, must now accept responsibility for making some difficult decisions. But it is not the end of everything. It is just the beginning of their search for trained, dedicated, and skilled people who can work with them in recharting the meaning and course of their lives. The woman may be tempted to use her situation to embarrass others who have hurt her—her parents perhaps or the man who impregnated her. Understandable though these feelings may be, the woman needs to learn more mature ways of resolving her rebellion, for she hurts herself all the more when she uses her pregnant condition as a weapon to expose, embarrass, and hurt others. Or the couple may attempt a "cover up" by getting a friend, a doctor, or a minister to arrange an adoption that is not legally secure, does not follow sound practice, and exploits the emotions of all concerned.

Things they should always do. The first thing a couple who think the woman may be pregnant should do is to go to a reputable physician for a thorough medical examination and advice. If she wants to protect herself in her own home community, she can find a reputable gynecologist by calling the hospital switchboard and asking who the gynecologists on the hospital staff are. Going to one of these doctors establishes the fact of pregnancy, or it may reveal that the man and woman are mistaken in their fears. At times both are quite ignorant of the real cause and signs of pregnancy. See Alan F. Guttmacher, *Pregnancy and Birth* (A Signet Book, The New American Library, Inc., n.d.). Also, Ruth I. Pierce has written a helpful volume, *Single and Pregnant,* published by Beacon Press, Inc., 25 Beacon Street, Boston, Mass. 02108. Determining whether or not the woman is really pregnant is the first thing a couple should do, or be advised to do.

The second thing they should do is to seek the aid of a competent spiritual adviser. This person may be a pastor or a wise and understanding laywoman or layman. The adviser should be a person who knows God in Christ as the heavenly Father and who knows what trouble is, who has a large measure of patience, who has the ability to keep confidences and to think before acting. The adviser should be a person whom the couple trust and preferably someone who has known one or both of them long enough to have proved his or her friendship. Preferably this person should have been trained in one of the great helping professions. This spiritual adviser may be the woman's Sunday school teacher, her immediate superior on her job, or the wife of the pastor. It may be the pastor himself, because pastors are being trained not to show shock, surprise, or hurt when people tell about their troubles.

The third thing the couple should do is to examine honestly *all* the alternatives they have available. They will be tempted to assume that there is only *one* alternative. To the contrary, there are several alternatives depending on personal ethics and the religious convictions of the couple. For example, the alternatives open to a Jewish couple, a Roman Catholic couple, and a Protestant couple may differ. More and more even middle-class single women are keeping their children, even though they are unmarried. Also, abortion is no longer an illegal procedure in some states. This is an alternative. Furthermore, adoption of the child into an already established family is an often used alternative. In those instances in which the pregnancy took place prior to marriage but because of the genuine devotion and the responsible commitment of the man and woman to each other, marriage itself is an alternative.

The fourth thing the couple should do or be advised to do is to get the vastly helpful professional guidance that is available. This couple needs help from agencies that have been especially set up for ministering to them. Several groups have provided institutions through which all the needs of couples in difficulty have been anticipated and can be considered and met wisely. They are as follows:

1. *The Children's Agencies*

Usually these are professional social-work agencies supported by the Community Chest, the United Fund, or whatever the title may be for the joint-fund drive of the social agencies of a city. Rural couples can, by going into the city nearest them, look in the telephone directory under "Children's Agency" and establish contact with this group of dedicated workers. The name and address of the national office is Child Welfare League of America, Inc., 44 East 23d Street, New York, N.Y. 10010. A couple in trouble can get personal advice by writing or calling here. Professional persons can order a directory of agencies from this address.

2. *Maternity Homes and Hospitals*

These agencies offer their services to women from all walks of life. They provide a haven where the woman can live and have proper care during the difficult months before and immediately after the delivery of her baby. If it is important for her to keep her pregnancy a secret, a woman may be sent to a maternity home or a hospital outside her own state.

Listed here are the names and central addresses for two of these services, which have homes and hospitals strategically located all over the United States. The couple may write or call the home or hospital nearest them.

Florence Crittenton Association of America, 608 South Dearborn Street, Chicago, Ill. 60605.
The Salvation Army, National Headquarters, 120 West 14th Street, New York, N.Y. 10011

Several religious denominations sponsor maternity homes and hospitals. The woman desiring maternal care in one of these institutions will find help from her minister, or through the denominational headquarters in her state.

These agencies provide trained, sympathetic, and dedicated persons to help a woman think through her destiny. She should not wait until the time of her delivery to seek them out. She should go immediately. They can help her with the difficult decision of whether to keep the baby or give it for adoption, whether to marry the man or not. If marriage is not a possibility, they can advise her how to earn her living and to rechart her course of life, how to understand the particular factors that led to her untimely pregnancy. Pastors, medical doctors, lawyers, and interested friends should be able to help a woman find one of these homes.

Skilled attention by a competent counselor can do much to help the father of the child toward a clear understanding of how he can best express his love and sense of responsibility in the given situation. Sentimental, hasty, and explosive solutions to this problem often result in permanent double damage.

3. Abortion Referral Services

One alternative to unwanted pregnancy for an increasing number of women, married and unmarried, is legal abortion. Though legal abortion is a physically safe medical procedure up until the time the third menstrual period has been missed, the couple will want to consider more than the physical well-being of the woman. By talking with a spiritual adviser, such as a trusted pastor, the couple can openly express potentially damaging feelings of guilt and despair. If the couple decide that, under God, abortion is the best alternative, they should arrange as early as possible for this medical procedure. *It should be done in a locality where abortion is legal.* If the woman has a doctor she sees regularly, she may ask him about getting an abortion. The couple may prefer to call their local hospital or medical school; they should ask for the Department of Obstetrics and Gynecology, and request the name of a recommended doctor. The city or county public health department, listed in the telephone book under the name of the city or county in which the couple lives, may also be able to recommend a doctor. The Planned Parenthood affiliate in the local community may be able to introduce the couple to a doctor who will help with the abortion and who will assist them in learning effective birth control measures to avoid unwanted pregnancy in the future.

The doctor consulted is not required to perform an abortion. He may, for example, decline for medical reasons. Some doctors may refuse as a matter of personal conscience. In that case, the couple may ask him for the name of another doctor who is known not to have conscientious objections to abortion. Once arranged, the abortion will take place in a hospital or an accredited medical facility. A concerned, understanding doctor will care for the woman following the actual medical procedure, and arrange for a checkup examination to take place two to three weeks after the abortion.

If the couple are sure that they will never want another pregnancy, they might want to consider voluntary sterilization. Information about this procedure is available through the family doctor or the doctor at the local family planning clinic. Sterilization is the most reliable method of birth control. This subject is discussed in

Chapter 6 of this book. For birth-control information or for abortion information and referral, the couple may write or call the Planned Parenthood Federation of America, Inc., 810 Seventh Avenue, New York, N.Y. 10019, for the address of their local family planning center.

The couple should be cautioned about abortion counseling specialists. Frequently these counselors take the position that abortion is the latest thing and everybody ought to have one. Their lack of understanding of the deepest feelings of the couple confronted with an unwanted pregnancy leads them to the assumption that abortion calls forth no more emotional involvement than any other simple medical procedure. The perplexed couple, however, know that their decision to seek an abortion calls into question eternal values. They need the patient understanding, care, and guidance of dedicated ministers, doctors, and other professional persons. Anything less belittles the value of human life.

9

Adopting Children

> Our heavenly Father, thou who hast adopted us
> as aliens and strangers into thy inheritance
> through Jesus Christ our Lord, we thank thee for
> the aspirations for parenthood that cause men
> and women to think of adoption. Help them to
> examine their hopes in the light of thy truth and
> the needs of the child to be loved for his own
> sake alone. May they love the child as an end
> within himself. Forbid that they shall use the
> child as a means to hide from their own weak-
> nesses. Grant them the patience of the parent-
> hood of us all, through Jesus Christ our Lord.
> Amen.

In spite of everything, some people cannot have children. You may seek to adopt a child. If you have de-
cided to adopt a baby, your first impulse is to let your
enthusiasm run away with you. Right then is when you
may become ruled by your feelings. You may not take
care to see to it that the baby you obtain is legally yours,
assured of all the rights and privileges that a natural-
born child of your own would have. You may be in such
a hurry that you overlook the subtle factors of matching
the child's intellectual and physical capacities to the expectations that people of your educational and social

level have of their children. Where can you get all this kind of guidance, and how can you be sure of what you are doing? Trained people have worked with the problems of adoption for years and are usually within easy driving distance of you.

There are many facts about the present-day scene in the adoption of children. If, for example, you are interested *only* in adopting a white, newborn infant, you may be in for a long wait. At the time of this writing (June, 1971) a news report says that in Kentucky, for example, there are 425 families who have been approved for adoption of a child through the Louisville office of the Kentucky Department of Child Welfare. They are waiting also. Additional families have applied and are waiting yet to be interviewed. The reason for this is twofold: first, a shortage of infants because of "the pill," legal abortions, and a change in attitudes toward parenthood outside wedlock. Second, the unwillingness of adoptive parents to consider a child who is older, or one who is of another race, or biracial, or one who is mildly retarded, handicapped, or suffering from known emotional problems.

To be forewarned by these realities is to be realistic about what you are doing, not discouraged. With these facts in mind, let us state a few guidelines for action.

First, avoid all persons who will "get you a baby quickly with no questions asked." Occasionally, professional persons—lawyers, doctors, ministers, etc.—freelance in this errand of mercy. Their good intentions and a lack of time to pay attention to all the complications that could arise often result in tragedy at worst and nagging insecurity over the years at best.

Second, you should read the excellent guidance material that is being published today. You can get some straight-from-the-shoulder help by reading the following books:

Brooks, Lee M., and Evelyn C., *Adventuring in Adoption*. University of North Carolina Press, 1939.

Carson, Ruth, *So You Want to Adopt a Baby*. Public Affairs Committee.

McWhinnie, Alexine M., *Adopted Children: How They Grow Up*. Humanities Press, Inc., 1968.

Rondell, Florence, and Michael, Ruth, *The Adopted Family*, 2 vols., rev. ed. Crown Publishers, Inc., 1965.

Spock, Benjamin, *Baby and Child Care*, Newly Revised and Enlarged Edition. Pocket Books, Inc., 1968. This book will tell you of the different kinds of situations that typically arise in the rearing of the average American child. Even though your child is adopted, it will not be exempt from these situations. Neither will you be exempt. When the going gets rough, you might think it is because the child is adopted! In reality it will be because all other children tend to have similar difficulties. Dr. Spock will help you to be a *bit* prepared for *some* of the surprises awaiting *every* parent. In his book you will find a discussion of the adoptive child.

Wasson, Valentina P., *The Chosen Baby*, rev. ed. J. B. Lippincott Company, 1950. A picture book for use in telling a child he is adopted.

If you want to read in more detail, get the books by Arnold Gesell and his associates. Their book *The Infant and Child in the Culture of Today* covers the first five years of a child's life. The second volume, *The Child from Five to Ten,* and a third volume, *Youth: The Years from Ten to Sixteen,* discuss just what the titles indicate. Frances L. Ilg and Louise Bates Ames in their book *Child Behavior* (Harper & Brothers, 1955) tell what to do about some of the typical problems that arise with children at certain age levels, in order to make subsequent stages smoother. More recent volumes are Fitzhugh Dodson's *How To Parent* (The New American Library, Inc., 1970) and Haim G. Ginott's *Between Parent and Child* (Avon Books, 1969).

Third, by the time you have studied along these lines, you will have tempered your enthusiasm with realism, your love with truth, and will or should be ready to walk steadily through the problems of adopting your child. Attention to legal problems is now of primary importance. Be informed. An excellent treatment of the legal factors is to be found in a short summary entitled *Essentials of Adoption Law and Procedure.* You can order this from the U.S. Children's Bureau, U.S. Department of Health, Education, and Welfare, Washington, D.C. 20201 (U.S. Children's Bureau Publication No. 331).

These legal problems are intensely important. Someone who lets you have her child without legal adoption can easily change her mind and want the baby back. Persons who permitted you to have their child under shady circumstances can demand money of you in return for letting you continue to keep the child. This may not cease with the coming of the child into your home. Demands may be repeated. Legal protection, out in the open, clearly recorded, is the only answer to these anxieties.

Fourth, *never try to adopt a child without going through the channels set up by an approved adoption agency.* Search until you find a good adoption agency to give you personal supervision in this process. The agency will help you to find a child who is matched to the intellectual level on which you will naturally expect your child to function, or will advise you clearly that the child cannot function at that level and give you the free choice of adjusting to a mentally retarded child. It will keep the identity of the real parents of the child concealed absolutely from you and keep your identity concealed absolutely from the real parents. Ways of doing this have been perfected, so that your chances of being confronted by the real parents will be extremely remote if not totally impossible. The agency will perfect the legal papers and give you absolute, incontrovertible legal right to the child. As surely as if the child were your natural-born child, he or she will be legally yours permanently. You will be given follow-up encouragement, guidance, and advice as you confront the problem of telling the child that he or she is adopted, as you encounter unexpected events such as the rejecting attitude of members of your family whom you have not seen in some time when they discover you have adopted a child. The caseworkers in these agencies have been especially trained in schools of social work to deal with problems that you have only begun to think about. They will be able to anticipate your feelings with a reassuring sense of understanding. Therefore, they will be your comrades on a radiant adventure of parenthood with your child. How can you get in touch with these people?

The Child Welfare League of America has member agencies all over the United States. Usually they are listed under the heading "Children's Agencies" in your telephone book. Call the one nearest you for an appointment. If you live in an area where there is no such agency listed, you can write to the national office at the following address and get the name of the agency nearest to you: Child Welfare League of America, Inc., 44 East 23d Street, New York, N.Y. 10010.

Another way to contact a good adoption agency is through the Children's Division of the Department of Public Welfare of your state. If you will send a letter to your state capital, addressed to this department, they can give you a complete list of agencies that might suit your needs. Or your local Council of Social Agencies, sometimes called the Health and Welfare Council, sometimes the United Fund, etc., will be able to refer you to a local adoption service. Homes and hospitals such as the Salvation Army and the Florence Crittenton group sponsor and often have some direct relationship to adoption agencies inasmuch as more than half the children available for adoption are mothered by unmarried women. These agencies can be contacted through their national offices: Florence Crittenton Association of America, 608 South Dearborn Street, Chicago, Ill. 60605; The Salvation Army, National Headquarters, 120 West 14th Street, New York, N.Y. 10011.

A new approach to adoption is the adoption of children who are either biracial or of another race. One Kentucky authority says that only five or six black children have been adopted within that state. There is the possibility of adopting children of races other than black. Nationwide contact between agencies makes it possible to move children into areas where race prejudice against them is not so great a problem as in Kentucky. One such agency is known as ARENA (Adoption Resource Exchange of North America). Holt (Holt

Adoption Agency Program, Inc., P.O. Box 95, Creswell, Ore. 97246) is an Oregon-based agency specializing in American-Asian children with a Korean or Vietnamese mother and an American father. We are told that adoption through Holt is a more expensive procedure than through some other agencies but quicker.

You may become impatient with the complicated procedures of adoption. Having babies takes time, straightening out the emotions of a young mother who cannot keep her child to the point where she decides to give it up takes time, and legal procedures take time. One of the best ways to look at this is to say that you would rather have the red tape in the hands of persons who can unravel it before you adopt the child than to become enmeshed in it yourself after you take the child home with you in a hurry and then suddenly discover that you are hopelessly involved. Another way of looking at it is to put yourself in the place of the mother who actually bore the child and is having to relinquish it. Would you be in a hurry to let the child go?

In all this stress and strain, your pastor can be your fellow pilgrim in your adventure of becoming a parent. He can join with you as an understanding friend as you learn how to pray for the consummation of your hopes. He can lead you to spiritual resources that will help you to grow in both wisdom and love for the child that will be yours. He can help you with the plans for the baptism if you are of a church that baptizes children, the religious nurture, and the bringing of the child into the hearts of the larger family of the church. In this act, you will enable the church to purify its own religion. The members, like you, will be exercising "religion that is pure and undefiled before God." They will be visiting the fatherless in their affliction! Do not miss this opportunity for fellowship with the church. It is composed of all kinds of parents—some of them adoptive parents like yourself; many of them parents of their own natural-born children; some of them, like Hester Prynne, parents of children born out of wedlock. All of them, like you, will have had their hearts turned to their children by the Father of our Lord Jesus Christ. You will remember that it was the heavenly Father who adopted his own Son out to a Palestinian girl and her husband, in order that through his love we in turn might become the children of our heavenly Father.

10
"Problem" Children

> Our heavenly Father, all of us are "problem" children to thee. We have through our rebellion necessitated the radical measures of thy healing love in Christ. Therefore help us to bear with the stresses in the lives of difficult children. Open our eyes as parents, pastors, teachers, social workers, doctors, and friends to our own tendency to reject children. Open our ears to what their behavior is trying to communicate to us of their real needs. Grant us thy firmness in bringing children up in the nurture and admonition of thy truth without discouraging them unduly. Amen.

The word "problem" is in quotation marks because it means different things to different parents. Overconscientious parents may be so fearful that their child will "turn out bad" that their very anxiety teaches the child to be that way. At the other extreme, apathetic, indifferent, and irresponsible parents may feel that "everything is O.K." until the child is involved in a delinquent act outside the home. It takes this to wake them up. But somewhere in between these extremes most parents find themselves working away at the baffling perplexities of parenthood. The plain need of every parent is the help of a few dependable, trained, and *objective* outsiders in the business of serving our children. Their help is available in most communities, large or small, city or rural. Several agencies are available upon whose help you may continually call. They are listed in the order of the seriousness of the problems that your child may present, with which they are equipped to deal. Taken all together, these persons form a community team with you and each other, dedicated to the service of your child. One of the first impulses you will have is to find something to read. Therefore, get Fitzhugh Dodson's *How To Parent* and Haim Ginott's books, *Between Parent and Child* and *Between Parent and Teenager*. Ask for the paperback editions.

Your most immediate resource is the *public-school teacher*. Public-school teachers spend more time with your child than anyone outside the home. They see him in relation to many children as well as to the authority of the law that requires him to attend school. They have an objective view of him at work and play in his larger world. They will rejoice at your taking the initiative to find out what they have learned about your child. They can, when specific problems arise with which you feel helpless to cope, give you some suggestions and compare notes with you about the successful ways they have found to deal with your child. Furthermore, you can ease their task by giving them background detail on your child that will help them to understand him better.

The *school guidance counselor* is a member of the administrative staff in most public schools. This person has received special training in order to help your child work through problems occurring at school. The guidance counselor will work with the teacher to devise a plan of instruction suited to your child's interest and abilities. You may help make your child's learning experience more enjoyable by calling the school guidance counselor and giving information about the adjustment problems your child is having at school.

The *school social worker* (or the visiting teacher) in many public-school systems works to establish good communication between the home and the school. By calling this person, you can often get real help for a child who has become a problem to himself and to others. The school social worker knows what resources are available within your community to help your child with specific problems.

The law requires school attendance. When children become truants the *attendance officer* enforces this law. Nevertheless, he is *not* an officer of the law. He is primarily concerned with being a friendly counselor of the child and his parents. Think of him this way. Truancy from school is a symptom of approaching seriousness in your child's situation. Take your attendance officer as a friend, a counselor, and a confidant. He can help you to understand your child and yourself better.

If your child continually violates the limits you have set, or if your patience is exhausted, call your local Family and Children's Agency for an appointment. The social workers at such an agency can offer to you their personal help in understanding the way your child's behavior problems are related to the life-style of your family. If you live in an area without such an agency, the local child welfare worker can offer much the same service. This social worker's name and telephone number are available through the office of your county judge.

Your child's *Sunday school teacher* may be the most

significant person in his life outside his home. The Sunday school teacher is not paid for his work. It is a labor of love. Often your child will feel more open to and less threatened by a good Sunday school teacher than he does by other adults. Stay in touch with this meaningful person and seek suggestions from him or her.

The pastor of your church also has a rich store of friendships in the community upon which he can draw in constructively aiding you with your child outside the home. If the child is without a father or mother, often the pastor's own family becomes a sort of substitute for that which is missing. The church in a very vital way fills in many gaps in the lives of needy persons. For instance, the child without brothers and sisters goes to the church before he goes to any other institution. He finds there play and work group relationships with children his own age. In fact, the spiritual by-products of consistent church attendance in an effective church fellowship all add up to rich resources for meeting your child's growth needs.

If the church has a *director of Christian education,* you should immediately become acquainted with that person. Such a person will give you a continuing guidance, can recommend good books, and can form group discussions with other parents which you may attend and where you may find specific encouragement and insight.

Once again your *family doctor* can be of service to you. A "problem" child can be "acting up" because of a real illness that is in the making. Your pediatrician can give you specific assistance on such difficulties as are discussed in the book by Nina Ridenaur, *Some Special Problems of Children: 2 to 5 Years* (National Association for Mental Health, 1949), and the book by Benjamin Spock, *The Pocket Book of Baby and Child Care*. David K. Bernhardt has a helpful recent book entitled *Being a Parent* (University of Toronto Press). Ask for it in paperback.

If real personality disorders are beginning to emerge, a *good pediatrician* can give remedial advice until he feels that clinic or private psychiatric help is indicated. Then he can put you in touch with the nearest child guidance clinic or with a private psychiatrist. The National Association for Mental Health, Inc., 10 Columbus Circle, New York, N.Y. 10019, publishes a nationwide listing of these clinics. It is entitled *Directory: Psychiatric Clinics and Other Resources in the United States* and includes a listing of facilities not only for children but also for adults. Also, they have a *Directory of Facilities for Mentally Ill Children in the United States* which lists the staff, the costs, the type of care, and the sponsoring organizations.

A *mentally ill child* is a very different child from a mentally retarded child. One is an illness of the whole person. The other is a deficiency of intelligence. The illness lies in the disturbance of ability to communicate and in breakdown of interpersonal relationships. Consequently, therapeutic help, usually consisting of play therapy, consultations with parents, the use of tranquilizing drugs, etc., is indicated for upset, continuously disturbed children. Your doctor can detect this and advise psychiatric help if you will give him the whole story of the child's behavior patterns.

Of course, the large majority of problem children are not mentally ill at all. They are "acting out" their feelings in all kinds of behavior that reflect impulsiveness, poor judgment, and a desire to see how much they can get away with before someone sets limits for them and takes them seriously. This is particularly true of adolescent boys and girls. Rudolph M. Wittenberg's *The Troubled Generation* (Association Press, 1967) is a wise and realistic book to read. Lillian Ambrosino has written a book entitled *Runaways* (Beacon Press, Inc., 1971), in which she studies ways of helping young persons who have run away from home. She has forty pages of nationwide listings of agencies that give almost around-the-clock attention to runaway boys and girls in different parts of the country.

Some children are so seriously ill mentally that they need institutional care. For instance, the Central State Hospital, Anchorage, Kentucky, has developed a special section of the hospital for the separate care of mentally sick children and another section for adolescents. You can check with your state Department of Mental Health for information on this. If you are in a place remote from larger cities, your county Board of Health or Department of Welfare can give you advice as to available care for a mentally sick child.

Some additional basic pamphlets and books to read may be of further help. You should order the publication list of the Child Study Association of America and of the Public Affairs Committee for a rather complete bibliography. Addresses for these and other agencies are given in Chapter 2 of this book in the section "How to Select Helpful Literature." The U.S. Government's Department of Health, Education, and Welfare, Washington, D.C. 20202, provides funds for the free distribution of many excellent pamphlets on the emotional growth of your children. Here are a few titles that are valuable:

When Your Child Asks About Sex, The Beginnings of Emotional Health, Some Special Problems of Children—thumb-sucking, bed-wetting, bad language, masturbation, destructiveness, etc. If your state has a department of mental health, these and many other titles are available from them upon request.

SMALL BOOKS TO BE USED AS GUIDES

Group for the Advancement of Psychiatry, *Normal Adolescence*. Scribner Library paperback, Charles Scribner's Sons, 1968.

Ilg, Frances L., and Ames, Louise Bates, *Child Behavior*. Harper & Brothers, 1955.

Oates, Wayne E., *On Becoming Children of God*. The Westminster Press, 1969.

Preston, George H., *The Substance of Mental Health*. Rinehart & Co., Inc., 1943.

Ribble, Margaret, *The Rights of Infants*, 2d ed. Columbia University Press, 1965.

11

Mental Retardation

PRAYER FOR A RETARDED CHILD

Dear Father, God, who drew for me
A clear-cut and determined destiny,
Open my heart to feel and see
The needs of those lost in mystery
Of unfulfillment undefined
Of childlikeness unconfined
To childhood's quick and passing years,
To simple laughter and fleeting tears.
Help me to shelter their need to grow
Where love is rich and time is slow.
Help me to open the quiet walk
Where the eternal child and his Father talk.
Help me to see that there opens a way
For some bit of fulfillment for him each day.
                                    —*Mary Jean Sweet.*

Well over two hundred different causes, syndromes, and diseases that are involved in mental retardation have been identified, yet in most cases the physicans cannot specifically diagnose any one of them. (*Mental Retardation: A Handbook for the Primary Physician,* The Report of the American Medical Association Conference on Mental Retardation, Chicago, April 9–11, 1964.) This sounds very different from our many superstitions about mental retardation, does it not? Mental retardation, fee-blemindedness, or whatever you call it, can happen in any family, rich or poor, regardless of social or educational background. No one is absolutely immune. Approximately 126,000 retarded persons are born annually, and approximately five million persons in the United States are retarded. Therefore, many people need clear guidance to find dependable help for their exceptional children. There are three groups of "children" among retarded persons. About 160,000 persons can be called "severely retarded," amounting to about 1 out of every 1,000 persons. They are so severely handicapped that they require constant supervision all their lives. Some cannot walk. Some cannot talk. All deserve the nursing care accorded a baby. The second group is the "moderately retarded" group, composed of about 640,000, or 4 out of each 1,000 persons. They develop at less than one half the normal rate of growth and development. They need continuous supervision, but they can learn self-care, acceptable behavior, and useful work under sheltered conditions.

The third group is the "mildly retarded" group. They comprise about 4,000,000 children and adults, or 25 out of every 1,000 Americans. They need special schooling. They can usually learn enough reading and arithmetic to meet daily needs. As youths and adults they require special help for vocational adjustment. Most can become self-supporting and capable of handling their own affairs. (*The Secret Child,* National Association for Retarded Children, 420 Lexington Ave., New York, N.Y.)

What can you do, where can you turn, upon whom can you depend, where can you find help when you need it for a retarded child?

First, you need to get a careful diagnosis of the child's condition. Do not let your sense of secrecy or unwillingness to face the real situation cause you to put your child in the group of the "mildly retarded" when he is really in need of more serious attention, or vice versa. Do not let your tendency to reject the child cause you to push a marginally dependent child into an institution just to get rid of him. Rather, secure good diagnostic help. Ask your general physician to refer you to a psychologist or a clinic for specialized diagnosis and advice. You can go directly to a child-guidance or mental-health clinic or to a child evaluation center yourself. A directory of the exact names and addresses of these clinics can be secured by writing to the National Association for Mental Health, 10 Columbus Circle, New York, N.Y. 10019. These persons can give your child careful neurological and psychological testing. The clinic usually has a staff of social workers, a psychological and medical staff, and a chaplain who will interview you and give you specific guidance concerning the limitations and potentialities of your child. Most adults are tempted to expect more of children than children are able to deliver in results, but yours will be a double temptation. These workers can help you to avoid expecting too much or too little from your child. But bear in mind that just "getting the facts" in an authoritative manner is not the whole of your needs in obtaining a diagnosis of your child. As Dr. Leo Kanner, a celebrated child psychiatrist, writes, "Parents are no longer dealt with merely as passive recipients of authoritatively presented wisdom, but as deeply concerned persons who can, and should, be prepared for the task of becoming understanding and active participants." (NOTE: This is a quotation from an article by

Leo Kanner, M.D., entitled "The Questions Asked by Parents," in *Children Limited,* April, 1956, p. 11. *Mental Retardation News* is the more recent monthly information service on the latest research discoveries and ways of dealing with mental retardation. It is a newspaper that binds parents together in common concern for the mentally retarded and is available from the National Association for Retarded Children.) Two pamphlets are useful for the parents of retarded children: *How to Provide for Their Future,* and *The Three Stages,* which is helpful in the parents' own self-understanding.

Second, if your child is in the first two groups named above, he may need some kind of institutional care, attention from a home-visitors service, a day-care center, or a sheltered workshop, especially if you have other children whose normal needs will be unmet if you attempt impossible things for this child. You will want to get some specific help as to the location, exact address, persons in charge, etc., of both public and private schools and homes for the retarded. The American Association on Mental Deficiency at 5201 Connecticut Avenue, N.W., Washington, D.C. 20015, can provide you at a small cost an up-to-date *Directory of Residential Facilities for the Mentally Retarded.*

Third, if your child is in the group of those who do *not* have to be cared for in an institution, it is highly important that you form close friendships with the teachers in the public, private, or specialized teaching institution which he attends. These teachers have had special training in meeting your child's needs. In fact, all parents should have this attitude toward their children's teachers, particularly public-school teachers. These are the royal priesthood of American children, and we should undergird their efforts and try to be better parents. Parents should insist on personally knowing the teachers of their children, and place their services at the teacher's disposal in every way that is useful. This, in the light of our all-too-skimpy religious education of children, is a way of recognizing the essentially Christian service that the teachers of young children render in the community.

Fourth, the parent of a retarded child, such as a mongoloid child, which involves a hereditary factor, will inevitably face the anxiety of having another child that is similarly retarded. Recently, techniques of examination of the mother in the earliest trimester of the pregnancy have been devised for predicting whether or not the child will be retarded. A child diagnostic and evaluation center in a university medical school can either do this for a family or send them to the right person in a nearby community. Here again must be faced the ethical decision of whether or not a mother at this early stage of pregnancy should have an abortion in order to prevent bringing a severely retarded child into the world.

Fifth, you cannot carry this deep concern of yours alone. Seek out other parents who are facing the same problem. As one parent put it:

> Time passed, we knew not how, and eventually brought with it a kind of healing numbness. We went about our daily work mechanically and without purpose. There was no ray of sunshine, no relief from the piled-up pain. And then one night I came to a meeting of the Parents' Group in that blessed old East Patterson Firehouse, and for the first time realized that I was not alone; that there were many others who had the same problems.

"Misery loves company"; but I never fully appreciated that until I joined the Parents' Group.

Write to the National Association for Retarded Children, 420 Lexington Avenue, New York, N.Y. 10017, or to their second address, 2709 Avenue E, East, Arlington, Tex. 76011, and ask for the name and address of the chapter nearest you. Ask them to send you their publications list, which will give you information that will help you to organize a group of the parents of retarded children. As a group you can sustain one another, interpret one another's feelings, and work on ways and means of meeting your children's needs and improving community services toward that end. For instance, what are the churches represented among you doing to give specialized religious education to your children? What is the state doing to improve institutional care of the completely dependent children? Can public relations and promotion effect changes in these things?

Furthermore, since the concentrated interest of President Kennedy and the Kennedy family in mental retardation, extensive resources have sprung up all over the United States for the care of retarded persons. Comprehensive mental health centers in your area are commissioned and subsidized by the federal and state governments to give expert attention to the needs of the mentally retarded. Look them up and ask for their assistance.

Finally, you need the courage that your pastor as a man of God can share with you when you permit him to face this problem with you. You will have deep questions of justice in relation to God. You will wonder how to pray, for your heart will be filled with groanings that cannot be uttered. You will feel times of loneliness and separation. You will very much need the interpretive wisdom of a dedicated, capable pastor. If your child is a perpetual child, and if as Jesus has said the faces of little children do always behold the glory of the Father, then you have access, through your child's face, to God in a strangely lasting way that others do not.

A READING LIST ON MENTAL RETARDATION

American Medical Association (535 South Dearborn Street, Chicago, Ill. 60610), *Mental Retardation: A Handbook for the Primary Physician.* 1965.

Buck, Pearl S., *The Child Who Never Grew.* John Day Co., Inc., 1950.

Caplan, Gerald, *Prevention of Mental Disorders in Children.* Basic Books, Inc., 1961.

Kirk, S. A., *et al., You and Your Retarded Child: A Manual for Parents of Retarded Children,* 2d ed. Pacific Books, 1968. Paperback.

Levinson, Abraham, *The Mentally Retarded Child,* rev. ed. John Day Co., Inc., 1965.

Lewis, Richard S., *et al., The Other Child: The Brain-injured Child,* 2d ed. Grune & Stratton, Inc., 1960.

Rogers, Dale E., *Angel Unaware.* Fleming H. Revell Company, 1953. Paperback.

Sarason, S. B., and Doris, John L., *Psychological Problems in Mental Deficiency,* 4th ed. Harper & Row, Publishers, Inc., 1969.

12

The Adolescent

> Our heavenly Father, we thank thee for the gift
> of life, for the joys and the ideals of adolescence.
> We pray for thy wisdom as these young people
> confront the decisions which will shape their
> present happiness and their future hopes. Grant
> to those whose guidance and friendship they seek
> a measure of thy patient understanding. Preserve
> the freedom of these young people to keep on ask-
> ing, to keep on seeking, and to keep on striving
> as they seek to understand their world, their
> friends, themselves, and their God. As they in-
> crease in wisdom and stature may they also
> increase in favor with thee and their fellowman,
> through Jesus Christ our brother and our Lord.
> Amen.

If you are between the ages of twelve and eighteen,
adolescence may be a time of happiness and joy for you.
The chances are, however, that you also have some
things that you consider problems. Moving from childhood to adulthood is a task that, in spite of the gladness,
can at times be painful and confusing. As one sixteen-
year-old boy said to his pastor, "Growing up is the hard-
est things a person has to do." The difficulties of adolescence may be focused in the questions you and your

friends ask. After all, these questions spring from your own real feelings. This chapter considers three such questions and offers some suggestions as to where help may be found.

WHAT IS HAPPENING TO ME?

Many changes are brought about in puberty—genital development, breast changes, changes of voice, the growth of pubic and facial hair. These changes make you concerned with the way you look to other people. You have discovered, perhaps painfully, that you are accepted or rejected by many people on the basis of your appearance. Friends and family may disagree on what constitutes acceptable appearance. The way you look may influence employment, the viewpoint of a friend's parents, or how a policeman is likely to treat you. Usually, appearance matters far more to you when you are around other young people than when you are with parents or other adults. For that reason, the latest fashions, current hair styles, a suntan, and well-proportioned physique are important to you. Few human bodies are perfect, and all are subject to disease and illness. When you as an adolescent become concerned about these very real "thorns of the flesh," help is available.

Frequently young persons are concerned about their weight. If you feel that you are overweight or underweight, a visit to your physician, whether a pediatrician or family doctor, is in order. He can give you advice about appropriate changes in exercise and recommend a diet for you. You should avoid putting yourself on a self-prescribed diet either to gain or to lose weight. Often such magic diets without medical advice fail to provide the necessary nutrition for your body during this time of growth. Your doctor is also the person to talk to about other physical concerns. Skin problems, dental problems, or problems with eyesight may be embarrassing to you. A good doctor will understand your embarrassment and listen to your concerns. If he feels a specialist is needed, he may recommend a skin specialist, a dentist, or an eye specialist.

Adolescents often ignore or disregard common symptoms of physical illness. If you are not in the best of health, your body has a way of sending you signals to alert you to potential problems. If you have lingering headaches, nausea, or sore throats, a slow-to-heal sore, or unusual tiredness, a diagnosis by the doctor may, in the long run, save time, trouble, and perhaps discomfort. Some young people have feelings of sexual inadequacy or deformity. Girls may have problems or fears connected with menstruation. Others, for good reason, become frightened at the possibility that they may have contracted a venereal disease. A caring doctor can be of help to you when you have such concerns. He not only will see to your physical needs but will also understand your feelings of shame, embarrassment, or guilt. He will protect your privacy and not tell what he knows without your permission.

If you think you have venereal disease, it is especially important to visit a doctor as soon as possible. These diseases can be treated effectively if you act promptly. If you prefer not to go to your family doctor for this particular problem, call the local general hospital. Many such hospitals have clinics especially designed to treat problems such as venereal diseases. If no such clinic is available, ask to see a staff doctor at the hospital. You will need to be specific when you tell him of your concern. Information about the symptoms of venereal disease is available through your city and county health department, the specialty clinic at your local hospital, or from your family doctor.

The American Medical Association makes available many reasonably priced pamphlets on such topics as fitness and sports, skin care and grooming, sex education, diet and nutrition, alcoholism and drug dependence. *Venereal Disease Is Still a World Problem, Approaching, Adulthood, Why Girls Menstruate, Contact Lenses, Something Can Be Done About Acne, Sunlight and the Skin, Why the Rise in Teenage Syphilis?* and *Why the Rise in Teenage Gonorrhea?* are just a few of the titles that may be of help to you. A complete list of these pamphlets will be sent to you upon request. Write to the American Medical Association, 535 North Dearborn Street, Chicago, Ill. 60610.

WHAT IS EXPECTED OF ME?

Adolescence is not only a time when you as a developing person become aware of your bodily image, but it is also a time of acute interest in what others expect of you. You as a young person must discover and evaluate each expectation. You may then be able to say, "That's me" or, "That's not me." You may, however, see contradiction in the expectation or conflict between two different expectations. In other words, as an adolescent you may often feel two ways in regard to what is expected. When these battles of loyalty arise, help is available.

The question of manners is important to many young

people. Perhaps you have felt uncomfortable with a group of friends your own age because you were not quite sure about socially acceptable manners. A special event at school such as a homecoming dance or a senior banquet can be a tense situation for the young person who is not sure what is expected in the way of manners. If you are invited to a friend's house for a meal, you may also feel uncomfortable. Even though you want to accept the invitation, you may be a little embarrassed because you are not sure about proper manners.

The best way to learn about manners is to ask a person whom you feel will understand. Your Sunday school teacher, a schoolteacher, the pastor's wife, or the pastor himself may be able to help. You might suggest that a group of young people get together for a few hours each week to learn and to practice good manners. *Seventeen,* a magazine for young women, has published a book on etiquette that may be useful to you. Your school or public librarian will help you locate this book.

Your friends may have other expectations of you. For example, going steady may be the thing everybody is doing in your group of friends. Not only do you feel the pressure to go steady but many of the people you would really like to date are going steady with someone else. Further pressure may be added by what your parents expect of you. They may disapprove of your dating one, and only one, person.

A dilemma such as this can make anyone feel very much alone. The best thing to do, of course, is to get your feelings in the open. You want your friends and your parents to know how you feel about the pressure and the expectations. However, the best thing to do is sometimes the most difficult. You may be able to clarify your feelings and receive encouragement by again talking with a trusted adult. This is not a way of ganging up against either your parents or your friends. It is a way of being fair to yourself.

Certain things are expected of you at school. Usually such things as assignments and requirements are made clear by the teacher, while rules and regulations are clarified by the principal. Even though you will not always like what is expected, you will know where you stand. The most important thing that is expected of you at school may not be very clear. *You are a student.* In other words, being a student has priority over whatever else you are. If you are on the student council, an athletic team, the yearbook staff, or the cheerleader squad, this is in addition, and secondary to, your role as a student.

If you are having difficulty as a student, help is available. Your guidance counselor can help you arrange a schedule of classes that will suit your needs, interest, and abilities. If you have problems in a particular class, you can usually talk to that teacher about your problems. Many teachers will listen and try to understand your difficulty. Their responsibility is not only to make assignments but also to help you complete them by making suggestions and recommendations. If you have difficulty in relating to a particular teacher, a talk with your guidance counselor, giving the facts, will do far more good than "putting teacher down" in front of your friends.

Your parents and other family members expect certain things of you. More than likely the family depends upon you to do some work around the house such as mowing the grass, carrying out the garbage, washing the car, or babysitting. The most important thing your family expects of you is not limited to any particular job. You are a member of the family. You have only one family and one set of parents, and they have only one son or daughter exactly like you. In other words, your family needs you, not just your work. You probably find yourself spending more and more time away from home. This means that the quality of time you have at home is increasingly important if the family relationships are to be sound. You may want to plan to be at home on special days—days that hold special meaning for one or more of your family members. For example, birthdays, Mother's Day, Father's Day, Thanksgiving, and Christmas are good times to plan to be at home. In addition to these days your family may decide, upon your suggestion, that every family member will keep one night a week open to spend with the family.

You may recently have become aware of the frailty of the relationships within your own family. If you feel that your family is having problems that cannot be resolved by the family alone, help is available. Seeking help is not a way of embarrassing your family; rather, it is a way of finding help for the whole family, including yourself. Do not hesitate to seek such help on your own initiative. Your pastor may be the person to choose as a family helper. He has contact with every member of the family and can help the family as a unit. He also knows other people whose wisdom and training can be added to his if you need them and give him your permission to get in touch with them. The local family and children's agency may be such a place. You can find the telephone number and address in the telephone directory under "Children's Agencies." Finally, if you are concerned about your relationship to your parents, you might give them a book to help increase their understanding of adolescents. Such books as: *Between Parent and Teenager,* by Haim G. Ginott (Avon Books); *On Becoming Children of God,* by Wayne E. Oates (The Westminster Press); and *Normal Adolescence* (Group for the Advancement of Psychiatry, Scribner Library) are all available in paperback. Perhaps you and your parents could discuss the ideas found in these writings.

HOW FAR CAN I GO?

The sudden bodily changes that occur in early adolescence give you, as a young person, the appearance of an adult. This causes others to increase their expectations of you. The fact that social and emotional development do not keep pace with physical growth puts the young person in a double bind. On the one hand, you may want certain aspects of life to remain as they have always been, while others expect you to function as an adult in those same areas. On the other hand, you may want adult freedom in areas in which society feels you are unable to assume mature responsibility. Furthermore, you may already have become acutely aware of contradictions in adult actions and adult expectations. The conflicts between wishes and expectations, desires and limitations, values and contradictions, may lead you to ask, "How far can I go?"

The law often limits how far you can go, at least legally. For example, a minimal driving age exists, with automobile insurance to pay. There is a minimum age for seeing some movies and for drinking in a bar. Your signature is not legally binding until you are twenty-one

years old. If you are a boy, you must register with the
Selective Service Board on your eighteenth birthday.
These limits are set by the lawmakers.

Your parents have probably set some ground rules too. If
you break a curfew thoughtlessly, keeping your parents
worrying and waiting, you may expect to spend next
weekend at home. If you drive the family car too fast,
your privilege of driving may be revoked by your parents for a reasonable time.

How far you can go is often determined by you. Sexual limits, for example, can be set only by you. If you
feel that sexual intercourse should be reserved for marriage, then you must set the limit. Decisions about whom
you date, where you go on a date, what you do while
there, are largely up to you, even though other people
may have advice or opinions. The results of your actions
often involve other people. For example, teen-age pregnancy usually involves the concern of the parents of the
girl and the boy.

Money and education may also impose limits as to
how far you can go. Your spending power is related to
your earning power. If you want to buy an expensive
item—an automobile, a camera, a musical instrument—
you may have to save the money you earn for several
months before the purchase can be made. You cannot
realistically expect your parents to subsidize your plans
for world travel or your own apartment. Jobs may be
difficult to find, especially the kind of job you want. Furthermore, your desire for a money-earning job may conflict with your educational plans. For example, your
plans may be to go to college, but the only work you
can find is full-time employment. Is it worth the sacrifice
required of study time to take the job?

How far you can go in the future may depend on how far you decide to go now. Your performance "record" has suddenly become crucial. Academic standing, behavior record, athletic performance, encounters with the law, and reputation in general can influence your dreams about the future. When the pressure of limits becomes a problem for you, look for help.

You may feel that there are so many limits that your freedom is completely gone. Your decision may be to violate the limits in rebellion or to become so afraid of the limits that you are immobilized. If you find yourself beyond the limits, "out in left field," or if you feel frozen, talk to a person whom you trust. A schoolteacher, a guidance counselor, your pastor, your next-door neighbor may be such a person. The first thing to do is to have your feelings clarified by an objective person.

Unusual stress may lead to what you consider to be an emergency situation. You may think of running away to a large city, getting drunk, or getting high on drugs as ways of providing relief. You may be tempted to seek a more permanent kind of escape through a quick marriage, or even suicide. In these times of intense pressure, it may be difficult to think of anyone you would normally consider trustworthy. For that reason, it is a good idea to keep an emergency list in your wallet or purse. Many cities now have a Crisis Control Center, a Suicide Prevention Center, or a Hot Line for teen-agers. These centers have a trustworthy person on duty twenty-four hours a day. In emergency situations they can be reached by calling the telephone operator and asking for the Center.

The second thing you will want to do is explore the alternatives. You may do this by reading a good book about the area giving you difficulty, or in talking with a person who is knowledgeable in that particular area. For example, if military service seems overwhelming to you, a good book to read is *Guide to the Draft,* by Arlo Tatum and Joseph S. Tuchinsky, 3d ed. (Beacon Press, Inc., 1970). You may then talk to a guidance counselor about the alternatives available to you. If you are confused as to what to do about sexual feelings, you might read *Living with Sex: The Student's Dilemma,* by Richard F. Hettlinger (The Seabury Press, Inc., 1966). You may want to talk with a teacher of sex education or with your own doctor. If you are going steady and are concerned about potential difficulties, the book *Teen Love, Teen Marriage,* edited by Jules Saltman (Grosset & Dunlap, Inc., Publishers, 1966), may help you. A talk with your pastor or with one of the organizations listed in Chapter 4 of this book will help you further to clarify your feelings.

Once you know the alternatives, you will be better able to make a decision. You may want to discuss this with the same person you talked to in the first place. A trusted counselor will stand by you as a friend, not only while you make the decision but as you see it through. For those who have difficulty talking to an adult about their deepest feelings, an understanding Roman Catholic priest has written a book that may be of help. It is *Why Am I Afraid to Tell You Who I Am?* by John Powell (Peacock Books, Angus Communications, 3505 North Ashland Avenue, Chicago, Ill. 60657).

The question, How far can I go? may be for you a religious question. Adolescence is the time when feelings and thoughts about religion undergo many changes. You will begin to realize more and more that simply to adopt the religion of your parents is not enough. Your faith must be yours alone. Do not hesitate to ask questions of God. After all, God has much to account for. Again, discuss your thoughts and feelings with a person you trust, a person who seems to have found some of the answers. Your pastor is a specialist in this part of your growth. He can enable you to sort through the religion of your childhood so that your faith may mature. Your pastor will suggest helpful passages of Scripture and other reading material, such as the paperback *Your God Is Too Small*, by J. B. Phillips (The Macmillan Company, 1961). This process of asking, discussing, reading, and meditation will help you begin to make one of the most important decisions of adolescence—deciding whose child you really are. Are you the child of your parents or an adopted child of God the Father?

13

The Draft

O God, our refuge and strength, we thank thee
that thou art the leader of all who trust in thee,
without whom nothing is strong, nothing is holy.
We pray for this young man facing the possibility
of military service. As he explores the alternatives
available to him, may he be reminded that ulti-
mate loyalty belongs to thee. Grant to him protection from panic and propaganda, as he makes
decisions regarding this portion of his life. May
those who love him and those who guide him
honor the integrity of his decisions. Give to us all,
Father, grace that we may cast away the works of
darkness and put upon us the armor of light. Deliver us from the evil of this age and restore to us
the peace of our Lord Jesus Christ. Amen.

Every male living in the United States and its territories, citizen or noncitizen, is required by law to register with the Selective Service System within five days
following his eighteenth birthday. If you are soon
to be eighteen years old, you should know that there is
no legal alternative to this requirement. You should not
assume, however, that your life is to be at the mercy
of the Selective Service System. The truth is that within
the limits defined by law the freedom to make decisions

regarding your own future is available. This chapter is written to apprise you of the alternatives and to guide you to helpful literature and resource persons. Our intention is not to persuade you to choose any one alternative. Rather, we encourage you to examine the alternatives, consult the resources, and make your own decision.

1. The first alternative available to you is to allow the Selective Service System to make your decisions for you. After registration you can simply wait for action by your local (permanent) draft board. You may receive, for the calendar year in which you become nineteen years old, a high lottery number which is not called. In that case you will not be required to serve in the military. You may be rejected by the military service for failure to meet physical, mental, or moral qualifications. Or you may be inducted and required to report for military service. These are all involuntary proceedings so far as you are concerned. If you decide to take your chances, all you need do is follow whatever orders you receive.

2. A second alternative is to serve in the Army, Navy, Air Force, or Marine Corps. If you perform military service, you will enter it in one of three ways. You may, of course, be inducted through Selective Service. You may expose yourself to the lottery and wait until you are drafted in the normal order. You may decide to end the wait to be drafted and volunteer *for induction* in order to get it over. If you enter military service in this way, you are in exactly the same situation as the man who is drafted.

A second way of entering military service is by volunteering directly for one of the branches of the Armed

Forces. More than three out of every four men in the Armed Forces enter in this way. If you enlist, ordinarily you must sign up for three or more years. However, you have the chance to choose which branch of the Armed Forces you will enter and perhaps to select your type of training and area of assignment. If you enlist, you will get the same pay and veteran's benefits as those who are drafted. You may, however, qualify for a commission as an officer by graduating from one of the military academies, taking advanced ROTC in college, or by qualifying for Officer Candidate School after you have entered the Armed Forces.

A third way of entering military service is to join the reserves of one of the Armed Forces, including the National Guard and Coast Guard. Each branch of the Armed Forces has a variety of programs that allow you to spend most of a six-year period in the Ready Reserve. Usually, soon after you enlist in a reserve unit you will be required to spend several months in full-time training or a longer period on active duty. Each state has National Guard programs with similar requirements. Ready Reserve members remain subject to call for active duty by the President, while National Guard members are subject to the call of the governor of the state, to deal with national disaster or civil disorder.

If you want to volunteer for military service, the best person to advise you about the military alternatives is a recruiter. All branches of the Armed Forces have recruiters and all are trained to sell their own branch of service. They will emphasize advantages and challenges but may say little about the frustrations and problems. For example, recruiters may promise training in the field you are interested in, or assignment overseas in the area of your choice, but you may be later disappointed if the program is closed or you do not meet the qualifications for it. Furthermore, most recruiters know more about active duty than about the reserves. The best way to get information about the reserve units is to visit those in your area and talk with the men in them. If you decide to volunteer for military service, the feelings of your family members will be involved in your decision. Discuss it with them and with your pastor. A trusted minister has access to the whole family and can care for the people you love while you are on active duty.

3. Another alternative is voluntary enlistment in the Public Health Service or in the Environmental Science Services Administration. The Public Health Service commissions doctors, dentists, medical specialists, pharmacists, social workers, and other persons whose training is related to health. Officers are assigned to hospitals, research laboratories, local health work, the Coast Guard, or the Bureau of Prisons. The Environmental Science Services Administration commissions officers to conduct scientific research and service. You must have at least a bachelor's degree with a major in science or technology to qualify for a commission as an officer. If you serve in either of these organizations, you will fulfill the requirements of the Selective Service System. Information is available by writing to the following addresses:

U.S. Public Health Services, Office of Personnel (OSG), 9000 Rockville Pike (NBOC No. 2), Bethesda, Md. 20014.

Chief, Commissioned Personnel Branch, Environmental Science Services Administration, Washington Science Center, Rockville, Md. 20852.

The placement office at your college or university may also have information regarding these organizations. You may be able to arrange for a personal interview with the Public Health Service or Environmental Science Services Administration officials through the placement director.

4. A fourth alternative is to maintain a deferred status through your twenty-sixth birthday. If you want to qualify for any deferment or prefer to pick your own time to perform military service, the basic principle to follow is to keep your local draft board informed promptly and in writing of any change in your situation that would entitle you to receive or maintain a deferred status. Generally, once you have initially qualified for and been granted a deferment and continue to maintain the status that was the basis for your deferment, there will be no grounds for reclassification. You must, however, keep your local draft board informed of the reasons for which you feel your deferred classification should be continued before the expiration of the deferment. If you maintain an occupational deferment or a hardship deferment through your twenty-sixth birthday, you will not be drafted unless you are a doctor or medical specialist. However, as of April 23, 1970, no new occupational deferments have been given. The undergraduate student deferment (II-S) automatically terminates when you reach your twenty-fourth birthday. If you are in the Peace Corps and receive induction orders, the Selective Service National Headquarters will normally postpone your reporting date until your initial tour of service is ended.

If you want to discuss your classification with your local draft board, you may request a personal appearance. Furthermore, you may want to appeal your classification if you feel the local board gave inadequate consideration to your situation. Beyond this appeal to the state board you may be entitled to a Presidential appeal. All such requests must be made within thirty days after your most recent classification card was mailed to you.

So-called draft counselors are available in many cities in the United States. Although the authors of this book are skeptical of any counselor with so narrow a range of interest and competence, we do acknowledge that some of these draft counselors have valuable information that may help you if you are seeking either a deferment or an exemption. Furthermore, these draft counselors usually can put you in touch with an attorney well informed on the laws regulating the Selective Service System. The name and address of the draft counseling service nearest you is available by writing: CCCO/An Agency for Military and Draft Counseling, 2016 Walnut Street, Philadelphia, Pa. 19103.

5. Exemption from military service is a fifth alternative. If you are a conscientious objector, the sole surviving son of your family, an alien not liable for military service, a minister or divinity student, or if you are judged to be physically, mentally, or administratively unable to perform military service, you may be exempted from the draft. If you feel you are eligible for an exemption, the burden of proof rests with you. As with the deferment classification, you must keep your local draft board promptly informed of any changes in your situation.

Of all Selective Service classifications, conscientious objection is probably the most difficult to define and to identify. If you have strong moral objections to killing in a war and to carrying arms, you may want to apply for the I-A-O classification. As an I-A-O you may be drafted but must be assigned to noncombatant duty. If you are opposed to any form of military service for moral reasons, you may want to apply for the I-O classification. As an I-O you may be ordered to spend two years in civilian service, approved by your local board.

A list of many employing agencies offering jobs suitable for alternative service entitled *Guide to Alternative Service* is available, for a small amount, from the National Interreligious Service Board for Conscientious Objectors, 550 Washington Building, 15th Street and New York Avenue, N.W., Washington, D.C. 20005. You should apply for either the I-A-O or the I-O classification as soon as you become aware of your moral conscientious objection to military service. Your objection must be based on deeply held moral, ethical, or spiritual beliefs. You must be opposed to participation in war in any form. Your claim must be sincere, not an expedient means to avoid military service. Your recognition and classification as a conscientious objector depends on these three requirements.

If you are the sole surviving son of a family, you may be exempted from military service. If your father or one or more of your brothers or sisters was killed in action or died as a result of injuries or disease incurred during military service, you may be eligible for exemption and should ask.

Aliens admitted to the United States for permanent residence are not normally exempt from military service because of their alien status. However, you may be exempt on the understanding that such exemption precludes your becoming a citizen of the United States.

You may also be exempt if you are a citizen of one of fifteen countries which have treaties with the United States providing for your exemption.

If you are a duly ordained or regular minister of religion, preaching and teaching the principles of your religion, and are recognized by your religion as a minister, you may be exempted. If you are preparing for the ministry under the direction of a recognized church, sect, or religious organization, or are pursuing a full-time course of instruction in a recognized theological or divinity school, you may also be exempt from military service. The minister officiating at your ordination and/or the registrar of your seminary can provide the necessary information to your local draft board at your request. Do not assume that this information will automatically be forwarded to the Selective Service. You must specifically ask that it be done.

You may be exempt from military service because of a physical, mental, or administrative condition. A complete listing of disqualifying defects is found in *Medical Fitness Standards for Appointment, Enlistment, and Induction* of Army regulations 40-501. This public document may be obtained from the Superintendent of Documents, Government Printing Office, Washington, D.C. 20402. If you have a condition listed in this document, you cannot serve in the Armed Forces except in case of war or national emergency.

You should notify your local draft board as soon as you become aware of a disqualifying condition. An interview with the medical adviser attached to your local board will be arranged. You may want to ask your own family doctor and hospital officials to prepare full reports of your condition for the interview with the medical adviser. If after you have been ordered to take a preinduction physical examination you become aware of a disqualifying condition, you should notify your local draft board and take all evidence you have from your own doctors, hospitals, and other sources. Since the pre-induction examination may be hasty, you should point out to the doctors that you have evidence of a disqualifying condition.

If your doctor and you disagree with the results of your preinduction physical examination, you should write immediately to the Surgeon, U.S. Army Recruiting Command, Hampton, Va. 23369. Explain why you believe further consideration of your condition is needed, sending copies of your medical evidence. If you are not satisfied with the results of this appeal, you may write to Chief, Physical Standards Division, Office of the Surgeon General, Department of the Army, Washington, D.C. 20315. Letters should be sent to these officials only if your condition is genuine and you support your claims with substantial evidence.

6. A final alternative available to you is illegal avoidance of induction. You may refuse to cooperate with the Selective Service System in any way because you oppose the system that drafts people. You may consider leaving the country and giving up your citizenship to avoid induction. This alternative also deserves careful consideration and consultation with professional persons. You may want to discuss this alternative with your parents openly and honestly. They will need to understand your feelings because their future, as well as your own, will be affected by your decision. You will want to consult a lawyer who is familiar with the Military Selective Service Act of 1967. Your failure to comply with the provi-

sions of this law will subject you to a maximum of five years imprisonment and/or a $10,000 fine. Your pastor may also be able to help you clarify your feelings about the issues at stake for you. He will not be judgmental but will hear you out and reflect to you his understanding of your dilemma.

These, then, are the alternatives. The choice is yours to make. However, in order to decide, you need complete, accurate information. The fact that the Selective Service laws and regulations are constantly undergoing review and revision complicates the task of finding up-to-date information. Furthermore, solid-rock reliable information is difficult to discover in the sea of propaganda connected with the draft. Two books may be valuable to you. *Curriculum Guide to the Draft* is published by the National Headquarters, Selective Service System, 1724 F Street, N.W., Washington, D.C. 20435. *Guide to the Draft*, 3d ed., was written by two draft counselors, Arlo Tatum and Joseph S. Tuchinsky, published by Beacon Press, Inc., Boston, Mass. 02108.

Armed Forces recruiters and draft counselors have information and advice that may be helpful to you. However, these counterparts are salesmen at heart. They tend to have their own ideas about what is best for you. Our suggestion at this point is to gather the information from every available source and utilize your own system of checks and balances in deciding what is best for you.

Information is available through the employees of the Selective Service System. However, this too may be slanted. They, also, are salesmen at heart. The local board clerks are frequently better informed than board members, especially regarding your file and status with the Selective Service. By writing to the Office of the

Director, Selective Service National Headquarters, 1724 F Street, N.W., Washington, D.C. 20435, you can request answers to general questions about the draft. Refer questions regarding appeal of your classification to the State Director, Selective Service State Headquarters, followed by the address for your state:

Alabama
474 S. Court St.
Montgomery 36104

Alaska
619 Fourth Ave.
Anchorage 99501

Arizona
522 N. Central Ave.
Phoenix 85004

Arkansas
700 W. Capitol
Little Rock 72201

California
805 I St.
Sacramento 95814

Colorado
New Customhouse
19th & California Sts.
Denver 80202

Connecticut
P.O. Box 1558
Hartford 06101

Delaware
3202 Kirkwood Highway
Wilmington 19808

District of Columbia
440 G St., N.W.
Washington 20001

Florida
19 McMillan St.
P.O. Box 1988
St. Augustine 32084

Georgia
901 Peachtree St., N.E.
Atlanta 30309

Hawaii
P.O. Box 4006
Honolulu, 96812

Idaho
550 W. Fort St.
Boise 83702

Illinois
405 E. Washington St.
Springfield 62701

Indiana
36 S. Pennsylvania St.
Indianapolis 46204

Iowa
Building 68,
Fort Des Moines
Des Moines 50315

Kansas
10th & Van Buren Sts.
Topeka 66612

Kentucky
220 Steele St.
Frankfort 40601

Louisiana
Building 601-5-A
4400 Dauphine St.
New Orleans 70140

Maine
Federal Bldg.
40 Western Ave.
Augusta 04330

Maryland
31 Hopkins Plaza
Baltimore 21201

Massachusetts
John F. Kennedy
Federal Bldg.
Boston 02203

Michigan
P.O. Box 626
Lansing 48903

Minnesota
180 E. Kellogg Blvd.
St. Paul 55101

Mississippi
4785 Interstate 55 North
Jackson, 39206

Missouri
411 Madison St.
Jefferson City 65101

Montana
P.O. Box 1183
Helena 59601

Nebraska
941 O St.
Lincoln 68508

Nevada
P.O. Box 644
Carson City 89701

New Hampshire
P.O. Box 427
Concord 03301

New Jersey
402 E. State St.
Trenton 08608

New Mexico
P.O. Box 5175
Santa Fe, 87501

New York City
26 Federal Plaza
New York 10007

New York State
441 Broadway
Albany 12207

North Carolina
P.O. Box 9513
Morgan St. Station
Raleigh 27603

North Dakota
P.O. Box 1417
Bismarck 58501

Ohio
85 Marconi Blvd.
Columbus 43215

Oklahoma
417 Post Office-
Courthouse Bldg.
Oklahoma City 73102

Oregon
P.O. Box 4288
Portland 97208

Pennsylvania
P.O. Box 1266
Harrisburg 17108

Rhode Island
1 Washington Ave.
Providence 02905

South Carolina
1801 Assembly St.
Columbia 29201

South Dakota
P.O. Box 1872
Rapid City 57701

Tennessee
1717 West End Bldg.
Nashville 37203

Texas
209 W. 9th St.
Austin 78701

Utah
102 Soldiers Circle
Fort Douglas 84113

Vermont
P.O. Box 308
Montpelier 05602

Virginia
400 N. 8th St.
Richmond 23240

Washington
Washington National
   Guard Armory
S. 10th & Yakima Sts.,
Tacoma 98405

West Virginia
Federal Office Building
Charleston 25301

Wisconsin
P.O. Box 2157
Madison 53701

Wyoming
P.O. Box 2186
Cheyenne 82001

14

The Drug Abuser

Our Father, when we see a fellow human being caught in the bondage of drug abuse, we remember our own weakness. We all need the deliverance of thy love. Teach us to move through seasons of boredom by the refreshing power of thy Holy Spirit. May the example of our Lord Jesus Christ, who refused drugs upon the cross, be for us encouragement to confront, rather than escape, the harsh realities of life. We believe that thy truth can set free those who are enslaved to any sin. May thy church seek that truth in our efforts to guide the despairing drug abuser into a life of hope. Amen.

Life brings to all of us times of boredom when the routine of day-to-day living resembles a "rat race." The pressures of school and parents, of work and family, or of time and money make life seem like a perpetual treadmill. In the loneliness of this seemingly intolerable life-style one alternative is to attempt escape through drugs. The businessman is tempted to take an extra tranquilizer; the weight-watcher considers increasing his or her dosage of diet pills; the soldier is urged by his buddies to smoke marijuana, while the student is encouraged to try LSD; the child in the inner city hears that sniffing glue and paint is fun; the factory worker is told about the peacefulness of heroin. When the alternative to use drugs is presented, many people decide that here at last is their salvation from the boredom and pressures of the treadmill. But what appears to be a chemical solution to their problems often becomes the catalyst for problem multiplication.

There are varying degrees and types of drug abuse, so no system of classification of drug abusers is without error. However, some distinctions can be made according to the function of drug abuse in the person's total life-style. The teen-ager who first smokes marijuana at a weekend "pot party," the college student who uses "pep pills" to keep him awake during examination week, and the husband who takes one of his wife's prescription sleeping pills are situational drug abusers. They make the initial decision to use drugs in order to facilitate enjoyment, comprehension, or sleep. Though the drug may be temporarily helpful, the situational drug abuser takes unnecessary risks when he "prescribes" his own medication. Experimentation of this sort is the first step toward drug dependency.

The habitual drug abuser is the person who has become physically or emotionally dependent upon a drug. His use of drugs is no longer peripheral to his life-style but has been incorporated as routine or ritual. Drug dependency manifests itself in a variety of ways because of differences in the effects of various drugs and the personalities of drug abusers. For example, the person dependent upon amphetamines may appear abnormally cheerful, hyperactive, nervous, or irritable, whereas the heroin addict may appear drunken, calm, inattentive, or apathetic. One sure symptom of the drug-dependent person is his intense craving for the drug. Such a person will often express his desire for the drug, not only as something he "wants," but also as something he "needs."

Drug abuse can cause many different kinds of problems. Perhaps you are faced with some of the troublesome by-products of drug abuse even now. If you take illicit drugs (hallucinogens, heroin, marijuana) or if you take legitimate drugs (amphetamines, barbiturates, codeine, morphine) without a physician's prescription, you may be plagued with guilt feelings and fear of arrest because you are violating the law. If you have habitually taken one of the more expensive black-market drugs such as heroin or cocaine, you probably experience financial anxiety each time the last "fix" begins to wear off. You may even have sold your furniture or resorted to earning money through theft, prostitution, or selling drugs yourself. If you have taken hallucinogens, you may occasionally have abnormal experiences. For example, a side effect of LSD may be frightening "flashbacks" in which the psychedelic event reoccurs without warning. Other psychoactive drugs, as well as LSD, may give rise to sensory abnormalities which in some situations may endanger your life. If you began smoking marijuana because you wanted the approval of your friends, you were bored with your routine, or you just wanted to have a good time, you may now find that the initial pleasures are not durable. In your most insightful moments you perhaps view your mood as intensified loneliness, heightened suspicion, or deeper despair. Furthermore, you may be ambivalent about whether to quit the habit or to begin using some stronger drug.

Habitual drug abuse slowly destroys interpersonal relationships. Family difficulties frequently accompany drug dependency. You may feel that problems within your family contributed to your abuse of drugs in the first place. Even so, your relationships with family members have probably not improved, but deteriorated, since you began depending on drugs instead of people. Perhaps you have noticed that your work in school or on the job is slipping in quantity and quality. You may have felt unspoken disapproval from teachers or your employer and dropped out of school or lost your job. Furthermore, drug abuse has probably become detrimental to your relationship to God. You may feel as though God is getting farther and farther away from you even though your problems and your loneliness are increasing. If you have had a religious experience while under the influence of drugs, it may well have been terrifying for you. More than likely you find yourself unable to pray. You may be convinced that God has forsaken you when you need the assurance of his forgiveness. The intimacy of meaningful interpersonal relationships with family, friends, and God is neglected in the deceptive games of drug experimentation and is lost in the withdrawal characteristic of drug dependency.

If drug abuse has caused problems for you and your family, whether you are drug dependent or not, chances are good that you would like to know where to go for help. You may feel that you are not worth the trouble or that your situation is hopeless. Your hope lies in your ability to ask for help with the assurance that under God there are those who will try to help you. There are people you can trust who have spent much of their lives preparing themselves to be helpful to you. The habitual "old things" of your life can be overcome, and you can become a new person. This change can come about only if you are willing to be honest with yourself, admitting that you need help with your drug problem, asking for that help from some caring person whom you trust.

Your medical doctor can help. He is trained to know drugs and their action upon your body. He can interpret for you the physical changes you may experience in drug abuse and give a realistic appraisal of any long-term effects. Furthermore, if more intensive medical care is indicated for you, your physician will be able to introduce you to a hospital, a clinic, or other treatment facility where you can receive the kind of help that is necessary. If you do not have a pastor, or if you are in a strange city, look in a telephone directory for the local Council of Churches. They will be glad to give you the name and telephone number of a concerned, well-trained pastor.

You will find friends you can trust at your local drug-abuse center. These centers are located in many cities and have as their primary purpose the prevention of drug abuse through distribution of reliable literature and presentation of educational programs. However, many of these agencies have a twenty-four-hour "hot line" telephone service and can arrange for transportation, lodging, and food on an emergency basis. The drug-abuse center will also be able to advise you where you can find continuing help with your drug problem.

If you are in a metropolitan area, a free clinic may be available to you to help you with your drug problem and related difficulties. Many free clinics provide medical, dental, psychiatric, and drug treatment on a first come, first served basis. Most free clinics operate twenty-four hours a day. Consult the telephone directory or call the local drug-abuse center to get the address and tele-

phone number of the free clinic nearest you. Below is
a partial listing of free clinics.

Berkeley Free Clinic
2418 Haste St.
Berkeley, Calif. 94704

Blackman's Free Medical
  Clinic
689 McAllister St.
San Francisco, Calif. 94101
Tel. (415) 563-7878

Bridge Back Free Clinic
4771 South Main St.
Los Angeles, Calif. 90037

Cincinnati Free Clinic, Inc.
2444 Vine St.
Cincinnati, Ohio 45219
Tel. (513) 241-7889

Dover Committee on
  Drug Abuse, Inc.
874 Monroe Terrace
Dover, Del. 19901
Tel. (302) 734-9940

The Free Clinic
2039 Cornell Rd.
Cleveland, Ohio 44106

Haight-Ashbury Free
  Medical Clinic
558 Clayton St.
San Francisco, Calif. 94117
Tel. (415) 431-1714

Los Angeles Free Clinic, Inc.
115 North Fairfax
Los Angeles, Calif. 90036
Tel. (213) 938-9141

The Medical Service
1 Walnut St.
Boston, Mass. 02108

Open Door Clinic
5012 Roosevelt Way, N.E.
Seattle, Wash. 98105
Tel. (206) 524-7404

Outside-In Aid Station
1240 S.W. Salmon St.
Portland, Oreg. 97205

San Diego Free Clinic
Community Crisis Center
3004 Imperial Ave.
San Diego, Calif. 92101

Waikiki Drug Clinic
319 Paokalani Ave.
Honolulu, Hawaii 96815
Tel. (808) 923-5102

Washington Free Clinic, Inc.
1556 Wisconsin Ave., N.W.
Washington, D.C. 20005
Tel. (202) 965-5476

This is a skimpy list because very few such clinics
exist. However, they are being established slowly but

surely as the drug problem reaches epidemic stages. Therefore, one should write to the following address for information if it is not afforded by the above list:

The National Clearinghouse
   for Mental Health Information
5454 Wisconsin Avenue
Chevy Chase, Md. 20015

If you are addicted to a narcotic such as heroin, cocaine, or morphine, you are both physically and emotionally dependent upon the drug. More than likely you realize that your purpose in life has been reduced to getting another "fix." Though your situation is serious, help is available to you. If you want to be free from addiction, you have two choices. Methadone maintenance programs are found in many states now. In this kind of program you will be given the synthetic drug methadone instead of the drug you are now taking. The switch to methadone will cause little discomfort. With methadone you will be able to function in a more normal way than in your present state of addiction. You will be able to work and to rest without the frantic search for more drugs. Perhaps your dosage of methadone will be gradually decreased until you are no longer addicted. A medical doctor or a pastor will be able to help you locate the nearest treatment center using the methadone program.

A second choice you have is to receive help from those who understand you best. In some states treatment programs for narcotic addicts are administered by ex-addicts. Who could better understand your fears and your despair than a fellow human being who has been in your condition? Though these programs demand withdrawal without medication, or "going cold turkey," the people who will stand by you are living witnesses to the fact that you can become a new person. Your drug-abuse center will be able to give you the name, address, and telephone number of the inpatient treatment home nearest you. Names to look for are Daytop Village, Matrix House, Odyssey House, Synanon, and Teen Challenge.

Before you go to any person or agency for help, you may want to read about drug abuse. Much literature has been published on this subject, but not all that has been written is worth your reading. The local drug-abuse center will have some helpful literature they can hand to you. The Public Information Branch of the National Institute of Mental Health (Chevy Chase, Md. 20015) will send to you a series of pamphlets on drugs subject to abuse. These pamphlets answer questions about individual drugs, their effects, and their hazards. The American Social Health Association (1740 Broadway, New York, N.Y. 10019) has a chart entitled *A Guide to Some Drugs Which Are Subject to Abuse.*

The American Medical Association at 535 North Dearborn Street, Chicago, Ill. 60610, has the following pamphlets which are authoritative and inexpensive: *The Crutch That Cripples: Drug Dependence; Amphetamines; Barbiturates; Glue Sniffing; LSD; Marijuana.*

Several directories are available which list by locality drug-abuse centers and other helping agencies and organizations. The Student Association for the Study of Hallucinogens (638 Pleasant Street, Beloit, Wis. 53511) has compiled a *Directory of Drug Information Groups* which is thorough and well organized. *The Drug Dilemma* (McGraw-Hill Book Company, Inc., 1969), by Dr. Sidney Cohen, is a paperback book written for you as well as for those who are available to help you with your drug problem. As of this date, the most recent, thorough, and well-balanced book for anyone to read about drugs is by Henlee H. Barnette, *The Drug Crisis and the Church* (The Westminster Press, 1971).

The wisdom of Hebrew Scriptures may be for you the kind of reading material you want. The prayers of the psalms, especially Psalms 13, 22, 31, 38, 51, 55, 69, 102, 130, 139, may become your prayers as you seek a way out of the pit and the snare of drug abuse.

15

The Problem Drinker

> Our Father, we sincerely want to know how to
> pray for those for whom alcohol has become mas-
> ter of their lives. Thou hast taught us to subdue
> the earth, but in many ways all of us are subdued
> by the fruits of the earth. Forgive us. Look with
> compassion particularly upon the alcoholic, his
> family, and his community. Relieve them all of
> fear of responsible love. By the wisdom of thy
> love, teach us the ways by which the household of
> faith may restore those who enter into life
> maimed. Amen.

Have you experienced a blackout of consciousness
from drinking? Do you sneak drinks? Do you intend to
take only one drink, and wind up cockeyed? Do you
have to make excuses for the amount you drink? Do you
attempt to control your drinking by shifting your times
and patterns of drinking? Have you "gone on the wagon"
yet? Do you throw away money while drinking, spending
it extravagantly, that is? Have you yet been on a weekend drunk? middle of the week drunks? daytime drunks?
Do you take a morning drink? Have you started going
on benders that are interfering with your work and family life? Do you experience acute and persistent remorse
about a binge? Do you have any uncontrollable resent-

ments? Have you picked a fight with anyone for no good reason at all? Have you become indifferent to the quality of the liquor, just so it does the trick of getting you drunk? Do you get the jitters or shakes, or whatever your pet name for it is, after drinking? Have you resorted to taking sedatives to quiet yourself after drinking? Have you been hospitalized for drinking? Have you lost a friend, working time, an advancement in your job, or your whole job as a result of drinking? Have you sworn off alcohol in the name of religion, expecting magic to take place? Have you thought and planned to leave town to get away from drinking? Have you started to drink all alone? Have you started to protect your supply of alcohol?

If you answer any one of these questions with yes, you are a problem drinker and need to admit it plainly to yourself. You need to admit to yourself and another person that your drinking is beyond control and that you need help.

Your loved ones—your husband, your wife, your mother, your brother, your sister—may be the kind of persons who help to make you alcoholic if you don't watch their good intentions. In order to keep you from learning from experience, to keep you from embarrassing yourself and them, they will pull you out of one jam after another that your drinking creates for you. They will become a crutch for your irresponsibility just as surely as the drinking dulls your awareness of the painfulness of that need to be adequate and whole.

Therefore, the beginning of help is to confess your need for help, that you are helpless. The sources for help with this problem must be sought in several different directions. Your *medical doctor* can help you get sobered up and give you medication to offset some of the effects of malnutrition, etc., that you may be experiencing. Also, it is very easy to become overexposed in cold weather, to be unaware of the real state of the temperature either in the weather or in your body. As a result, you can contract as dangerous a disease as pneumonia without knowing it. Left untreated, pneumonia is a ruthless killer of people. You can die of it in a comparatively short time. If anyone suggests that you take antabuse, a drug to make you aversive to and repelled by alcohol, do not take it unless it is by the advice of your physician. This drug should never be taken except under the supervision of a physician.

Your *pastor* can serve you well by being a steady but gentle guide as you work your way back to drink-free days. He does not expect religion to act like magic for you. As a fellow human being who knows what suffering is and what it means to fail, he can remind you of the presence of God, cut down your isolation, and provide a release by listening to you when pressure begins to build you toward another drink. Your local *Family Service Organization* or state or county Department of Health can lead you to the rehabilitation programs for alcoholics now operative in most states.

Of course, before you go to any of these persons, you may feel the need to read on the subject of alcoholism and yet not know where to turn for reading help. Some continuing sources for literature on this subject are:

The National Council on Alcoholism, 2 Park Avenue, New York, N.Y. 10016. The Council publishes pamphlet and tract material that has been tested and proved useful. For instance, such titles as *How to Know an Alcoholic, What the General Practitioner Can Do About*

Alcoholism, and *Alcoholics Can Be Helped* are examples.

Alcoholics Anonymous Publishing, Inc., P.O. Box 1980, Grand Central Annex, New York, N.Y. 10017. This organization has useful pamphlets such as *The A.A. Tradition, The Alcoholic Husband, The Alcoholic Wife, Freed Slave of Drink.* A card written to either of these two organizations will bring literature of a very helpful nature.

Two books will give special help: Howard J. Clinebell, Jr., *Understanding and Counseling the Alcoholic,* rev. ed. (Abingdon Press, 1968); and *Alcoholics Anonymous,* rev. ed. (Alcoholics Anonymous Publishing, Inc., 1957).

Some excellent and inexpensive pamphlets are available through the National Council on Alcoholism, Inc.: Joan Jackson, *The Adjustment of the Family to the Crisis of Alcoholism;* Marty Mann, *How to Know an Alcoholic;* A. L. Blakeslee, *Alcoholism: A Sickness that Can Be Beaten;* Ruth Fox, M.D., *What Can Be Done About Alcoholism?;* Morris Weeks, *Thirteen Steps to Alcoholism.* An extensive research publication in the area of the nature and treatment of alcoholism is the *Quarterly Journal of Studies on Alcohol,* published by the Rutgers Center of Alcohol Studies, New Brunswick, N.J. 08902.

Remember that your doctor, your pastor, and others in your community can lead you to additional sources of help. Many persons in this country are taking a deep interest in the care of persons afflicted with the alcohol habit. The National Council on Alcoholism, Inc., is the national organization for information on developments and activities in the field of alcoholism, and disseminates the latest scientific and medical findings in this field. It also guides and stimulates the establishment of community programs on alcoholism. Literature is available;

write for the price list. Also, this organization can lead you to the local committees on alcoholism that are available for consultation in the various areas throughout the United States and Canada, as well as the outpatient alcoholism clinics for the treatment of alcoholism. Many of the local committees have fully developed information centers. One of the major goals of the national committee is to help the local committees develop similar information centers.

In addition to these agencies, one of the important resources on the treatment of the alcoholic is, of course, Alcoholics Anonymous, The Alcoholic Foundation, Inc., P.O. Box 1980, Grand Central Annex, New York, N.Y. 10017. There are over five thousand AA groups in this country, Canada, and abroad, for which the above office is the clearinghouse. The Alcoholic Foundation will be delighted to refer any pastor to groups in his immediate vicinity. Or groups in any given local area may be reached by simply looking in the telephone directory under "Alcoholics Anonymous."

Alcoholics Anonymous is a fellowship of men and women who share their experience, strength, and hope with each other that they may solve their common problem and help others to recover from alcoholism. The only requirement for membership is an honest desire to stop drinking. AA has no dues or fees. It is not allied with any sect, denomination, political organization, or institution, does not wish to engage in any controversy, neither endorses nor opposes any causes. The primary purpose of its members is to stay sober and help other alcoholics achieve sobriety.

Auxiliary to the AA are Al-Anon and Al-A-Teen groups. They are composed of the spouses of alcoholics in the case of the Al-Anon, and the sons and/or daughters of alcoholics in the case of Al-A-Teens. Al-Anon Family Groups Headquarters, Inc., at 125 East 23d Street, New York, N.Y. 10010, is the place you should write to get literature and information about groups near you.

COMPREHENSIVE MENTAL HEALTH CENTERS

Since the first edition of this book, the vast network of Comprehensive Mental Health Centers, many of which are in small towns and villages, has been established. Alcoholism rehabilitation, treatment, and prevention is one of the jobs of these centers. They are often walk-in clinics, that is, you can just walk in and ask for and get help. Look in your telephone book for their addresses and go ask for help. If you are too sick to do this for yourself, ask your doctor or your minister to call them for you. The Comprehensive Mental Health Centers will gear their program in with that of Alcoholics Anonymous if you wish. In other words, you can have the advantage of *both* services. Do something about this *now*.

16
Mental Illness

Regard, O Lord, with thy Fatherly compassion, all who are disquieted and tense, who cannot lose themselves either in happy work by day or in restful sleep by night, who looking within do not know themselves and looking to thee do not find thee. Lead them, we pray thee, out of clangor into quietude, out of futility into usefulness, out of despair into the sure serenity of truth. Teach them to believe that thou art faithful, and that thy love hopeth all things and endureth all things; that all darkness of the world, even the inner blackness of the soul, cannot quench one small candle of fidelity. Give them of thy perspective, thy humor, and thy gift of tranquillity and poise. Be so patient with them that they may learn to be patient with themselves; so firm that they may lean on thee; so persistent in leading, that they may venture out and find pasture in the sunny fields of thy Kingdom, where all who follow thy shepherding may find gladness and delight; in the name of the earth's most calm and daring Son, Word of God and Master of men, our Savior, Jesus Christ. Amen.   (*John Wallace Suter.*)

Everyone has a few eccentric habits and occasional cranky spells. But when crankiness interferes with work, family living, and especially when it becomes an unreasonable burden to others, the person is beginning to need help for emotional difficulties. Marked and prolonged changes in a person's typical pattern of life are trouble signals for help with an emerging mental illness. Such changes may be sudden. They may occur slowly and almost unnoticed for a while. Nevertheless a discernible change takes place. The person may begin to live in an imaginary world, separate from the lives of others, refusing to relate to others, or suddenly develop extreme and "hard-to-understand" religious ideas, enthusiasms, and behaviors. He or she may have pronounced and unreasonable suspicions of others, feeling persecuted by them. He or she may get in such a deep "spell" of the "blues" that he or she cannot talk or work. He or she may suffer severe indecision, especially over little details. On the other hand, the person may suddenly swing upward in his or her mood and be so elated that you cannot keep up with the train of thought. Or a patient may insist that he or she is ill when actually medical examinations reveal nothing wrong. He or she may be quite sleepless over a long period of time with no apparent cause. Loss of interest in appearance, remaining unkempt, unbathed, and without changing clothes regularly, may be symptoms. The person may hear or see things that are obviously hallucinations. He or she may threaten his or her own life or that of others. He or she may do any, many, or all of these things.

Such a person needs careful diagnosis through a process of medical and social examination. You should confer with your medical doctor. Tell him what you have observed about your loved one that has caused you to think that he might need help with an emotional problem. Also, you need the aid and comfort that your family pastor can give you at this time. Ministers trained in seminaries since World War II, and also ministers who have had military chaplaincy experience, have had a measure of training in helping persons to find the right kind of assistance when they have emotional problems. In any event, the pastor can afford spiritual fortification and the comradeship of an understanding friend in these times of confusion and stress. If you had a surgical operation, you would want your pastor for yourself and your family. Let it be so in this case too.

By all means avoid the quacks who prey on the desire of some to hide their mental illnesses, and who extract money from them without giving or being qualified to give real help. "Head bumpers," "hand holders," star-gazers, fortune-tellers and swamis, and numerous other titles have been used by such phonies. They should be avoided absolutely. Use the measuring guides set forth in Chapter 2 to locate a counselor. If in doubt, go to the regional office of the Veterans Administration, the Y.M.C.A., Y.M.H.A., the public-school principal, the head of the department of psychology in a nearby college or university, or to the Council of Social Agencies, or United Fund, United Appeal, or Community Chest in your area. Any of these groups can tell you the best place to go if you do not have access to a pastor or a general physician.

You will want to read some dependable literature. A helpful book by George H. Preston, *The Substance of Mental Health* (Rinehart & Co., Inc., 1946), gives a wholesome approach to your problem. Also, Edith M. Stern has written a book entitled *Mental Illness: A Guide for the Family,* 5th ed. (Harper & Row, Publishers, Inc., 1968). Public Affairs Pamphlet No. 172, entitled *When Mental Illness Strikes Your Family,* by Kathleen Doyle, and Pamphlet No. 228, *New Medicines for the Mind,* by Gilbert Cant, are unusually informative. These last two pamphlets dispel fears, answer questions, and clarify decisions that the family of a mentally ill person faces.

You must be aware that there are two procedures in getting help for a mentally disturbed person, voluntary and involuntary. If the person is unwilling to cooperate and get the help that he needs, then sometimes it is wise to use legal procedures in having the patient committed to a hospital. This calls for the advice and written opinion of at least two physicians in most states; therefore, you should confer with your doctor about the best way to do this. You should always be frank and honest with the patient about such procedures. To deceive the person is a real injustice and is quite harmful, sometimes forming a block to successful therapy.

You will raise some vital questions about the religious aspects of your problem or that of your loved one. If you are a Roman Catholic or related to a Roman Catholic, then William Christian Bier (ed.), *Conscience: Its Freedom and Limitations* (Fordham University Press, 1971), will provide you with a basic understanding. Protestants will find the book by Wayne E. Oates, *When Religion Gets Sick* (The Westminster Press, 1970), to be an extensive and adequate treatment of the problems.

You will be tempted to avoid the treatment you need by feeling that all psychiatric help is too expensive for you. This is a popular error. As research, education, and service have progressed, more and more reasonable resources for your treatment are being provided. The fact remains that all medical care is expensive, and the longer the term of illness, the more expensive it is. This is true of surgery and psychiatry particularly. You should move along several different lines to get the help, along with the personal counseling of your general physician and your pastor. You can go to the *public institutions* of your county and state for help. Although these hospitals have been inadequate in the past, both federal and state governments are making enough improvements to justify your confidence in the hospitals. Many state hospitals today are well staffed. More and more of them have full-time, clinically trained chaplains as well as other members of the "healing team." Recoveries are occurring at an increasingly rapid rate, especially since the discovery of newer therapies. If you are a veteran, you can count on excellent psychiatric care through the Veterans Administration hospitals. You should contact your regional VA office immediately about the facilities of their hospitals.

Another way to canvass your situation before going to a psychiatrist is to go to a *Family Service Organization,* usually listed under that title in your telephone book. These agencies are staffed with competent social workers who have been trained to give careful diagnostic attention to whether a member of your family needs psychiatric treatment. They are also aware of the psychiatric resources of your own local community and can lead you to the persons and institutions where you can obtain help that is in keeping with your income. Many minor emotional maladjustments can be dealt with by these workers and the time of psychiatrists can be saved to deal with the more serious kinds of difficulties that people in your community have to carry.

The National Association for Mental Health, 10 Columbus Circle, New York, N.Y. 10019, publishes a directory of the psychiatric facilities that are in existence all over the United States. So does the National Clearing House for Mental Health Information at 5454 Wisconsin Avenue, Chevy Chase, Md. 20015. You can order either of these directories and get the guidance you want by consulting their listings. The resources are so extensive that the publication of them here is not possible. Simply by addressing a note to these organizations, pastors, families, and institutions of all kinds can have this reference work at a small expense.

The choice of a private psychiatrist is a very real problem to the mentally disturbed person and his family. The main thing for you to look for here is a *good doctor*. Do not expect him to be a theologian or to do the work that is legitimately that of the minister. The important thing is that the doctor be thoroughly trained and capable of handling the illness of the patient, whose religious convictions he will approach with respect and sensitivity, neither rejecting wholesale nor approving all his religious ideas.

The doctor should be approved as a member of the American Psychiatric Association, having passed the Board examinations. He should have been in residence for extensive training in a hospital approved for psychiatric training. He should be accepted by the medical society of your local group of physicians. Your general physician, your pastor, and your local Board of Health can help you find the necessary information. The directory of the American Psychiatric Association, which can be consulted through your local physician, will give you the exact status of the particular doctor you are considering, or lead you to a doctor about whom you may not yet have learned.

You may be considering psychoanalysis, which is a

highly specialized branch of psychiatry. If this is true, you should by all means read the book by Karen Horney entitled *Are You Considering Psychoanalysis?* (W. W. Norton & Company, Inc., 1946). The various schools or emphases in psychoanalysis are discussed factually and sympathetically here, and the communication is addressed directly to the person considering the type of therapy. You should be warned that many people pose as "analysts" who have not been adequately trained. The various institutes of psychoanalysis are located in the larger cities of this country—New York, Washington, Chicago, etc. The therapy requires three to five interviews a week lasting from two to five years. This is intensive, expensive, and detailed therapy. It calls for a good deal of rearranging of a person's life simply to afford the time and money for the therapy. In the long run it is better to do that in some cases than it is to have a whole life permanently hindered by crippling illnesses. The addresses of the institutes of psychoanalysis are as follows:

American Institute for Psychoanalysis, 329 East 62d Street, New York, N.Y. 10021.
The Institute for Psychoanalysis, 108 North Michigan Avenue, Chicago, Ill. 60601.
Los Angeles Institute for Psychoanalysis, 344 North Bedford Drive, Beverly Hills, Calif. 90210.
New York Psychoanalytic Society, 245 East 82d Street, New York, N.Y. 10028.
Psychoanalytic Clinic for Training and Research—Columbia University, 722 West 168th Street, New York, N.Y. 10032.
Washington School of Psychiatry, 1610 New Hampshire Avenue, N.W., Washington, D.C. 20009.

Since the first writing of this book, however, several breakthroughs in the care of the mentally ill have been made. More varied resources are available. For example, the use of psychiatric drugs in treatment has enabled increasing numbers of persons to be treated on an outpatient basis who formerly had to be hospitalized. Even when patients are hospitalized, chemotherapy has shortened the length of many patients' hospitalization. Newer types of psychotherapy have shortened the processes of psychoanalysis as well.

Furthermore, the release of large amounts of federal and state funds for the development of regional mental health centers, commonly identified as Comprehensive Mental Health Centers, is revolutionary in concept, although it is a difficult concept to get into practical action. By writing to the National Clearinghouse for Mental Health Information at the National Institute of Mental Health, 5454 Wisconsin Avenue, Chevy Chase, Md. 20015, you can, for a modest cost, buy a copy of *The Mental Health Directory*. This gives a complete listing of addresses, telephones, areas served, etc., of all psychiatric facilities in the United States.

17
Suicide *

Eternal God, our creator and redeemer, we thank thee for making us in thine own image. Thou hast not made us in vain but dost love us with an everlasting love even when we are unable to love ourselves. When we fall into the pit of despair only to feel alone and far away from thee, we ask, O God, for patience to be lifted up. For the person contemplating suicide for reason of fear or guilt or anger, we ask thee to calm his fear, to forgive his guilt, and to hear his anger. May the decision confronting this person be made in the knowledge that Christ died that we might have life. It is in that hope that we are saved. Amen.

If you are considering killing yourself, there are several things you should do before you decide to die.

1. Pick up the telephone and call somebody—a suicide prevention center, a hospital, a doctor, a minister, a neighbor, the police station. The telephone operator can put you in touch with such a person if you do not have the number.

---

* We are indebted to Chaplain Sloan Lister, of the Woodhaven Medical Services, 8101 Dixie Highway, Louisville, Ky. 40272, for much of the data in this section.

2. Give the person your full name and address. Tell them of your plans for suicide—how, when, where, why.

3. Talk about whatever comes to your mind—your current crisis, your diminishing reasons for wanting to live, your unexpressed anger, your loneliness.

4. Talk about the person who has hurt you. Give their name, address, and relationship to you.

5. Arrange to see a professional person as soon as possible. This may be the person you call, someone they suggest, or a person you trust.

To read that there are things you should do before you decide to die may make you angry. Good. Feel free to write of your anger to either of us. Our addresses are given on p. 10. For one reason or another you have not expressed your anger. Perhaps you feel that to be angry is childish or selfish or impolite or sinful. Anger is none of these. In and of itself anger is a quite normal human feeling. It has constructive potential as well as destructive possibilities. If you want to learn about the creative value of your anger and how to use it as a means of helping, rather than hurting, yourself and others, follow the five steps above.

Another feeling you may be experiencing now is loneliness. Chances are that you are alone as you read these words. Even if you are in an airport, a bookstore, or a public library, you probably feel very much alone. The crisis that gave rise to your thoughts of suicide may have led to your loneliness. If you have recently lost your job, suffered a major failure, experienced the death of a person you loved very much, or finalized a divorce, you are likely to feel that no one cares whether you live or die.

There are those who care about you. The five steps above will put you in touch with such a person. You are worth the help that is available to you.

Your wish to die has not come upon you suddenly. It has been developing for some time. By the same token, your wish to live has not suddenly disappeared. Though at present your wish to die may be unusually strong, your wish to live is still active. Your ambivalence—that is, your two-way feelings—are confusing. For example, you may feel both love and hate for the same person. You may imagine that, like Tom Sawyer, you will be able to enjoy your own funeral. That is just not so. Your mixed feelings are confusing and stress-producing. By following the five steps listed in the first paragraph you will be able to begin to clarify your feelings and sort through the confusion of your wishes.

You may feel as if no one can understand your distress. The following prayer from the Bible may be helpful to you:

> Save me, O God!
> For the waters have come up to my neck.
> I sink in deep mire,
>   where there is no foothold;
> I have come into deep waters,
>   and the flood sweeps over me.
> I am weary with my crying;
>   my throat is parched.
> My eyes grow dim
>   with waiting for my God.
> More in number than the hairs of my
>   head
>   are those who hate me without
>   cause;

mighty are those who would destroy
    me,
    those who attack me with lies.
What I did not steal
    must I now restore?
O God, thou knowest my folly;
    the wrongs I have done are not
        hidden from thee.

Let not those who hope in thee be put
    to shame through me,
    O Lord God of hosts;
let not those who seek thee be
    brought to dishonor through me,
    O God of Israel.
For it is for thy sake that I have borne
    reproach,
    that shame has covered my face.
I have become a stranger to my
    brethren,
    an alien to my mother's sons. . . .

But as for me, my prayer is to thee,
    O Lord.
    At an acceptable time, O God,
    in the abundance of thy steadfast
        love answer me.
With thy faithful help rescue me
    from sinking in the mire;
let me be delivered from my enemies
    and from the deep waters.
Let not the flood sweep over me,
    or the deep swallow me up,
    or the pit close its mouth over
        me.

Answer me, O Lord, for thy steadfast
        love is good;
    according to thy abundant mercy,
        turn to me.
Hide not thy face from thy servant;
    For I am in distress, make haste to
        answer me.
Draw near to me, redeem me,
    set me free because of my enemies!

Thou knowest my reproach,
    and my shame and my dishonor;
    my foes are all known to thee.
Insults have broken my heart,
    so that I am in despair.
I looked for pity, but there was none;
    and for comforters, but I found none. . . .

But I am afflicted and in pain;
    let thy salvation, O God, set me on
        high!
                    —*Psalm 69:1–8, 13–20, 29.*

SUICIDE PREVENTION CENTERS

By leaps and bounds help is coming your way from the
suicide prevention centers which are rapidly being established in many localities. The National Institute of Mental Health has the following listings. If you have difficulty, because a phone number has been changed, ask
your operator to help you reach the suicide prevention
center in your area.

ALABAMA

Florence
Suicide Prevention and
    Emergency Service of the
    Muscle Shoals Mental
    Health Center. Tel. (205)
    764-3431
24-hour emergency tele-
    phone service. Profession-
    al staff.

ARIZONA

Phoenix
Emergency Mental Health
    Service of Maricopa
    County
2214 N. Central Ave. Tel.
    (602) 254-5303
24-hour emergency psychia-
    tric service, special atten-
    tion to suicide. Profes-
    sional staff.

Tucson
Suicide Prevention Center
1930 E. Sixth St. Tel. (602)
    792-1616
24-hour information and re-
    ferral service. Staff consists
    of nonprofessionals and vol-
    unteers; some professional
    consultation is offered.

CALIFORNIA

Bakersfield
Marilyn Adams Suicide Pre-
    vention Center of Bakers-
    field, Inc.
P.O. Box 1298. Tel. (805)
    325-1232

24-hour answering service.
    Professional and nonpro-
    fessional staff.

Berkeley
Suicide Prevention of Ala-
    meda County, Inc.
P.O. Box 9102. Tel. (415)
    849-2212
24-hour emergency tele-
    phone service. Profes-
    sional and nonprofes-
    sional staff.

Carmel
Suicide Prevention Center
P.O. Box 1904. Tel. (408)
    624-1415
24-hour answering service
    with nonprofessional vol-
    unteers; professional back-
    up.

Davis
Suicide Prevention Answer-
    ing Service
1620 Anderson Rd. Tel.
    (916) 756-5000
24-hour call-in referral ser-
    vice for Yolo County.
    Professional and nonpro-
    fessional staff.

Fresno
Crisis Intervention Service,
    or HET (Help in Emo-
    tional Trouble)
760 W. Nielson Ave. Tel.
    (209) 485-1432
24-hour answering service.
    Professional and nonpro-
    fessional staff.

Hayward
Hope for Youth (Youth
Counseling and Suicide
Prevention of Southern
Alameda County)
24718 Mission Blvd. Tel.
(415) 582-4673
Anonymous telephone coun-
seling for youth from 8
P.M. until midnight,
Thursday, Friday, and
Saturday nights. Staffed
with trained volunteers
with professional backup.

Imperial Beach
Crisis Clinic
455 Palm Ave. Tel. (714)
424-3941
24-hour answering service.
Professional staff.

Long Beach
Suicide Prevention Service,
Memorial Hospital
2801 Atlantic Blvd. Tel.
(213) 595-2353
24-hour answering service.
Service is given by the
clergy. Psychiatric and
psychological consultation
available.

Los Angeles
Help Line Telephone Clinic
The Los Angeles Baptist
City Mission Society
427 W. Fifth St. Suite 524.
Tel. (213) 626-1231
Service available 9 A.M. to

10 P.M. by lay volunteers.
Referrals.

Operation Bootstrap, Inc.
(Learn, Baby, Learn)
4171 S. Central Ave. Tel.
(213) 232-2129 and
232-2120
Community program set up
to "help people in any
way needed."

Suicide Prevention Center
2521 W. Pico Blvd. Tel.
(213) 381-5111
24-hour evaluation and referral service. Professional
and nonprofessional staff.
Research and training
facilities.

Mountain View
Suicide Prevention Answering Service
Psychiatric Unit of El Ca-
mino Hospital
2500 Grant Rd. Tel. (415)
916-8131
24-hour telephone service
with calls received by
anyone on duty.

Orange
Crisis Intervention Center
(Orange County Mental
Health Association)
101 Manchester Ave. Tel.
(714) 633-9393
24-hour service, week days
only. Professional staff
and trained volunteers

take daytime calls; registered nurses answer at night. Medical Center hospital facilities available; referrals to appropriate community agencies.

Pacoima
Golden State Community Mental Health Center
1160 Eldridge Ave. Tel. (213) 800-1111
Inpatient, outpatient, partial hospitalization (day care), 24-hour emergency, and community consultation.

Palm Springs
Suicide-Crisis Intervention Center
Desert Mental Health Association
590 S. Indian Ave. Tel. (714) 346-9502
24-hour answering service with professional and nonprofessional volunteers.

Palo Alto
Emergency Service, Psychiatric Clinic, Palo Alto–Stanford Hospital Center, Stanford University School of Medicine
300 Pasteur Dr. Tel. (415) 321-1200
24-hour emergency service, manned by first-year residents.

Pasadena
Medical Health Center
1815 N. Fair Oaks Ave. Tel. (213) 798-0907
Answering and walk-in service during weekday working hours. Volunteers are both professional and nonprofessional.

Sacramento
Suicide Prevention Service of Sacramento County, Inc.
2007 "O" St., Suite D. Tel. (916) 444-2255
24-hour answering service with nonprofessional volunteers and professional backup. Referral to community agencies.

San Francisco
Center for Special Problems
San Francisco City and County Department of Public Health.
2107 Van Ness Ave. (at Pacific Ave.). Tel. (415) 558-4801
Professionals, nonprofessionals, and volunteers comprise staff. Offers multiservices and extensive referral service.

San Francisco Suicide Prevention, Inc.
307 Twelfth Ave. Tel. (415) 221-1424
24-hour telephone service

answered by volunteers; professional supervision. Referrals to community agencies.

San Jose
Suicide and Crisis Service
Santa Clara County Mental Health Association in cooperation with Santa Clara County Mental Health Services.
645 S. Bascom Ave. Tel. (408) 287-2424
24-hour answering service by professional and nonprofessional volunteers. Referrals to community agencies.

San Mateo
Peninsula Suicide Prevention, Inc.
San Mateo County Mental Health Association
18 Second Ave., Room 211. Tel. (415) 344-2533
24-hour telephone service with nonprofessional volunteers. Psychiatric and psychological consultation.

Santa Cruz
Suicide Prevention Service
350 Mission St. Tel. (408) 426-2342 or 423-6700
Professionals and nonprofessionals handle calls. Answering service takes calls and refers them to

workers. Volunteers nonprofessional. Psychiatrists and ministers on backup calls. Referrals to agencies where necessary.

Stockton
Life Line, Inc.
914 N. Center St., Suite 6. Tel. (209) 466-2961
Telephone counseling service staffed primarily by volunteers with professional backup. Referrals to community agencies.

Vallejo
Suicide Prevention Center (Solano County Unit)
2417 Spring Rd. Tel. (707) 643-2555
24-hour telephone answering service. Staffed by nonprofessional volunteers during the week; ministers usually cover on weekends. Backup by clergy and professionals. Referrals to community agencies.

Ventura
Suicide Prevention Center
Ventura County Mental Health Association
4900 Telegraph Rd., Suite 95. Tel. (805) 648-2444
24-hour telephone answering service. Daytime calls are transferred to Mental Health Department;

other hours to the home of the volunteer. Referral service.

Walnut Creek
Contra Costa Suicide Prevention Service
Contra Costa County Mental Health Association
1510 Second Ave. Tel. (415) 939-3232
24-hour telephone answering service refers calls to volunteers who have professional backup. Referral service.

COLORADO

Colorado Springs
Suicide Referral Service of El Paso County, Inc.
Tel. (303) 471-4357
24-hour answering service. Staffed by volunteers.

Denver
Emergency Psychiatric Service
University of Colorado Medical Center
4200 E. Ninth Ave. Tel. (303) 394-8484
24-hour service. Offers telephone service plus diagnostic and evaluative services and crisis therapy. The suicide prevention services are incorporated in the separate Emergency Psychiatric Service.

Suicide Prevention Clinic
Hospital Chaplaincy Commission
2459 S. Ash. Tel. (303) 757-3731 (days) and 789-3073 (nights)
24-hour service

Psychiatric Emergency Services (Denver General Hospital)
West 6th Ave. and Cherokee St. Tel. (303) 244-6835 and 244-6969
24-hour answering service and walk-in service. Referrals to appropriate agencies.

Pueblo
Pueblo Suicide Prevention Center
151 N. Central Main. Tel. (303) 544-1133
24-hour telephone service. Nonprofessional volunteers and backup resources of clergymen, lawyers, physicians, and other professionals. Referrals, if necessary, and follow-up to see referrals are kept.

CONNECTICUT

Middletown
Help Line
Connecticut Valley Hospital
Middletown. Tel. (203) 347-8611

24-hour telephone and walk-in service. Staffed by professionals and nonprofessionals. Sponsored by State of Connecticut.

DISTRICT OF COLUMBIA

Washington
Suicide Prevention and Emergency Mental Health Consultation
D.C. Department of Public Health
801 N. Capitol St. Tel. (202) 659-5222
Mental health consultation and referral service.

DELAWARE

New Castle
Psychiatric Emergency Service of Delaware State Hospital. Tel. (301) 658-1366
24-hour answering and walk-in service, emergency home visits. Trained volunteers and professionals.

FLORIDA

Cocoa Beach
Suicide Prevention Center of Brevard County
Brevard Guidance Clinic
P.O. Box 1251, Cocoa, Fla. Tel. (904) 783-5555
Professional consultants and volunteer associates, 24-hour service.

Jacksonville
Suicide Prevention Center of Jacksonville
2627 Riverside Ave. Tel. (904) 384-6488
24-hour answering service with professional and non-professional volunteers.

Miami
F.R.I.E.N.D.S.
Dade County. Tel. (305) FR 4-3637
Nonprofessional, no professional supervision.

Life Line
Mental Health Association of Dade County, Inc.
30 S. E. Eighth St. Tel. (305) 379-2611
24-hour service, staffed by volunteers with professional backup. Daytime service is given at the Mental Health Association Building; evening calls are routed to volunteers. Referral service.

Orlando
We Care, Inc.
Mental Health Association of Orange County
608 Mariposa Ave. Tel. (305) 241-3329
24-hour telephone answering service. Volunteer

counselors answer the
phone backed up by pro-
fessionals.

Rockledge
Emergency Mental Health
  Service
Brevard County Mental
  Health Center
1235 S. Florida Ave. Tel.
  (305) 784-2433
24-hour telephone answering
  service, adult walk-in
  clinic; staffed by nonprofessional volunteers with
  backup by professionals.
  Referrals made to com-
  munity agencies.

St. Petersburg
Pinellas County Mental
  Health Emergency Service
6170 Central Ave. Tel.
  (813) 347-0392
24-hour telephone answer-
  ing service, staffed by
  social workers; referrals
  made to the adult mental
  health clinic; visiting service is offered.

Tampa
Suicide Prevention Center of
  Hillsborough County
P.O. Box 15674. Tel. (813)
  872-6054
24-hour telephone answering
  service, staffed by trained
  volunteers.

GEORGIA

Atlanta
Fulton-DeKalb Emergency
  Mental Health Center
99 Butler St. S.W. Tel.
  (404) 572-2626
24-hour telephone service
  with use of medical and
  psychiatric facilities at
  Grady Hospital. Profes-
  sional and nonprofessional
  volunteers are used.

IDAHO

Pocatello
Crisis Telephone
Bannock County Mental
  Health Center
807 E. Wyeth. Tel. (208)
  233-4357
24-hour service. Trained
  volunteers with profes-
  sional backup.

ILLINOIS

Champaign
Suicide Prevention Center
Adler Zone Center
2204 S. Griffith Dr. Tel.
  (217) 359-4141
24-hour telephone answer-
  ing service, staffed by professionals and nonprofessionals. Referrals are made
  to community agencies.

Chicago
Crisis Intervention Program
Charles F. Read Zone Center
4200 N. Oak Ave. Tel.
  (312) 794-3609
24-hour service. Interdisci-
plinary staff consists of
professional and nonpro-
fessional people. Referral
to other agencies when
appropriate.

Call for Help Clinic
1439 S. Michigan Ave. Tel.
  (312) 939-2860
Pilot project, 8 hours per
day. Professional staff.

Quincy
Suicide Prevention Service
Adams County Mental
  Health Association
520 S. 4th St. Tel. (217)
  222-1166
24-hour telephone service
plus walk-in; professional
personnel.

IOWA

Keokuk
Keokuk Mental Health Cen-
ter of Lee County.
Tel. (319) 524-3873
24-hour answering service.

KANSAS

Kansas City
Wyandotte County Suicide
  Prevention Center
Wyandotte County Guid-
ance Center, Inc.

250 N. 17th St. Tel. (913)
  371-7171
24-hour emergency service
using professionals from
the Guidance Center and
University of Kansas
Medical Center.

Garden City
Emergency Answering Ser-
vice (Area Mental Health
Center)
156 Gardendale. Tel. (316)
  276-7689
24-hour answering service
with professional staff;
psychiatric consultation.
Referrals to community
agencies.

Wichita
Suicide Prevention Service
  (Mental Health Clinic)
1900 E. Ninth St. Tel.
  (316) 262-2202
24-hour answering service
with professional volun-
teers and backup.

KENTUCKY

Louisville
Crisis Center
240 E. Madison St. Tel.
  (502) 589-4313
24-hour emergency service.

MAINE

Bath-Brunswick
Bath-Brunswick Mental
  Health Association
Tel. (207) 443-3300
24-hour answering service

Portland
Rescue, Inc.
Tel. (207) 774-2767
24-hour service for potential
suicides and alcoholics.

MARYLAND

Baltimore
Inner City Community
Mental Health Center
Program—Crisis Inter-
vention Service
The Psychiatric Institute,
University of Maryland
645 W. Redwood St. Tel.
(301) 955-8737
24-hour service with professional staff; functions as
a comprehensive mental
health facility.

MASSACHUSETTS

Boston
Rescue, Inc.
115 S. Hampton St. Tel.
(617) 426-6600
24-hour service with professional and nonprofessional
volunteers; backup by
Boston City Hospital
Psychiatric Department.
Mobile unit. Call No.
BOS-YJ-8-4242.

Worcester
Rescue, Inc.
Branch of Rescue, Inc.,
Boston. Tel. (617) 756-
1100

MICHIGAN

Ann Arbor
Washtenaw County Com-
munity Mental Health
Center
220 E. Huron. Tel. (313)
761-9830
24-hour service; professional
staff.

Detroit
Suicide Prevention Center
Community Psychiatry,
Detroit General Hospital
1151 Taylor. Tel. (313)
875-5466

Holland
Hope College Suicide Pre-
vention Center. Tel. (616)
396-HELP
24-hour coverage. Profes-
sional staff.

MINNESOTA

Minneapolis
Suicide Prevention Service
Hennepin County General
Hospital
5th and Portland S.
Tel. (612) 330-7777,
330-7650 (daytime)
24-hour telephone counseling service, including referral to and from other
county agencies, treat-
ment by hospital psychia-
tric facilities and follow-
up. Staffed by both pro-

fessional and nonprofessional persons.

MISSOURI

St. Joseph
Suicide Prevention Service
P.O. Box 263. Tel. (816)
AD 2-1655
24-hour emergency service
sponsored by the St.
Joseph State Mental Hospital and the St. Joseph
Mental Health Association. Staff made up of
professionals and volunteers.

St. Louis
Suicide Prevention, Inc.
1118 Hampton Ave. Tel.
(314) 388-2800
24-hour answering service
with professional and nonprofessional volunteer
staff. Sponsored by the
Mental Health Association of St. Louis (a separate unit).

NEBRASKA

Omaha
Personal Crisis Service
424 S. 40th St. Tel. (402)
391-3733
24-hour telephone and referral service. Staffed by
volunteer workers made
up of professionals and
nonprofessionals. Spon-

sored by Eastern Nebraska Mental Health
Association.

NEVADA

Reno
Crisis Call Center
Room 206, Mack Social
Science Building, University of Nevada. Tel.
(702) 784-6666
24-hour service. Staffed by
nonprofessional volunteers
backed by professionals.
Service is part of the Psychological Service Center,
University of Nevada.

NEW HAMPSHIRE

Berlin
North Country Mental
Health Clinic
227 Main St. Tel. (603)
752-4431
24-hour service. The clinic
handles calls on weekdays and an answering
service provides the name
of an on-call staff member
at nights and on weekends. Professional backup
and referral service.

NEW JERSEY

Hammonton
Suicide Prevention Telephone Service
Ancora State Hospital. Tel.

(609) 561-1234
24-hour answering service.
Staffed by professionals.

Marlboro
Emergency Telephone Service
Marlboro State Hospital. Tel. (201) 549-6000
Serves as afterhours auxiliary to Middlesex County Mental Health Emergencies Service. Staffed by residents in training and professionals. Referrals are made to the control center at Roosevelt Hospital Annex.

Metuchen
Middlesex County Mental Health Emergencies Service
Roosevelt Hospital Annex (Outpatient Section). Tel. (201) 549-6000
24-hour service. Night calls are bridged to Marlboro State Hospital. Professional and counseling help is offered and 24-hour walk-in service is in effect.

Perth Amboy
Raritan Bay Mental Health Center
Middlesex County Mental Health Association
591 Brace Ave. Tel. (201) 549-6000
24-hour telephone service from central switchboard with night calls handled by Marlboro State Hospital staff. Staffed by professionals and psychiatric residents. Associated with Perth Amboy General Hospital. Referral service to Middlesex County only.

Southeastern New Jersey
Suicide Prevention Telephone Service
Ancora State Hospital, Hammonton. Tel. (609) 561-1700
24-hour general crisis service; all psychiatric staff.

NEW MEXICO

Albuquerque
Suicide Prevention and Crisis Center of Albuquerque, Inc.
P.O. Box 727. Tel. (505) 247-2244
24-hour telephone service. Professional and nonprofessional volunteers.

Las Cruces
Crisis Center
200 Boutz Rd. Tel. (505) 524-9241
24-hour answering service with nonprofessional volunteers and professional backup.

192

NEW YORK

Brooklyn
Suicide Prevention Service
Emergency Psychiatric
  Treatment Service
Kings County Psychiatric
  Hospital, 606 Winthrop
  St. Tel. (212) 462-3322
24-hour telephone service is
  an extension of hospital's
  EPTS; phone has a special
  tone which alerts those on
  duty to emergency calls.
  Professional on duty who
  makes arrangements for
  ambulatory or hospital
  treatment.

Buffalo
Suicide Prevention Center
Citizens for Mental Health,
  1361 Main St. Tel. (716)
  886-7188
The Center is staffed by
  nonprofessionals; an advisory board of professionals offers backup.

Suicide-Prevention in Crisis
  Service, Inc.
Community Welfare Council,
  350 Genesee Bldg. Tel.
  (716) 852-8750

East Meadow
Meadowbrook Hospital
  Suicide Prevention Service
Meadowbrook Hospital,
  P.O. Box 175. Tel. (516)

538-3111 or 538-3112
24-hour service staffed by
  professionals and nonprofessionals. Offers full
  range of psychiatric treatment resources.

Long Island
Meadowbrook Hospital Sui-
  cide Prevention Service
Meadowbrook Hospital,
  P.O. Box 175, East Mea-
  dow, N.Y. Tel. (516)
  538-3111 or 538-3112

New York City
National Save-A-Life
  League, Inc.
20 W. 43d St. Tel. (212)
  687-2142
24-hour service with nonprofessional volunteers.
  Professional consultation
  available.

White Plains
Suicide Prevention Service
Mental Health Association
  of Westchester County,
  Inc.
29 Sterling Ave. Tel. (914)
  946-0121
24-hour central answering
  service with daytime calls
  accepted during the week
  by the SPS; nights by
  New Hospital; weekends
  and holidays by High
  Point Hospital. SPS calls
  are handled by psychiatric
  social workers; senior staff

members and residents at
the hospitals.

NORTH CAROLINA

Durham
Mental Health Clinic Crisis
Center
300 E. Main St. Tel. (919)
688-4366

Greensboro
Crisis Control Center, Inc.
P.O. Box 735. Tel. (919)
275-2852
24-hour telephone crisis service. Staffed by trained
volunteers, backed by
professionals. Referrals to
community agencies.

Jacksonville
Onslow County Mental
Health Center
255 Wilmington Highway
Tel. (919) 347-5118

Roanoke Rapids
Suicide Prevention Service
Halifax County Mental
Health Association and
Halifax County Health
Department. Tel. (919)
537-2909
24-hour telephone service.
Calls are answered by
police department opera-
tor and relayed to a counselor who gets in touch
with the caller. Profes-
sional backup and re-
ferral service.

Sanford
Suicide Prevention Service
P.O. Box 2428. Tel. (919)
776-5431
Lee County Mental Health
Clinic, 106 W. Main
Street. Tel. (919) 775-
4129
24-hour telephone answering
service by professionals
and nonprofessionals.
Mental Health Clinic
answers phone during
weekdays; night and
weekend service is staffed
by ministers, with clinic
staff in supervisory capacity and as referral service.

NORTH DAKOTA

Bismarck
Suicide Prevention and
Psychiatric Emergency
Service
Psychiatric Unit of St. Alex-
ius Hospital
Ninth and Thayer. Tel.
(701) 255-4124
24-hour telephone service.
Phone has a special tone
so it can be distinguished
in nurses' station and on
residential section of
ward. Professionals and
nonprofessionals assist.
Sponsored by Burleigh
County Mental Health
Association.

Fargo

Suicide Prevention Center
Ward Two-East, The Neuro-
psychiatric Institute Hospital. Tel (701) 234-4357
(H-E-L-P)
24-hour service, answered
by registered nurses on
staff of the psychiatric
ward. Ministers in the area
are available for referral
and visiting services.

Grand Forks

Emergency Service (North-
east Mental Health and
Retardation Center)
509 S. Third St. Tel. (701)
772-7268
24-hour answering service
with professional staff.

OHIO

Ashtabula

Suicide Control Center
Mental Health Clinic of
Ashtabula County
505 W. 46th St. Tel. (216)
993-6111
24-hour service. Clinic staff
answers phone during
workday week; other calls
go to the emergency
room of the local general
hospital.

Cleveland

Psychiatric Emergency Evaluation and Referral Ser-
vice
Suicide Prevention Center

10539 Carnegie Ave. Tel.
(216) 229-4545
24-hour service coordinating
all emergency facilities.
Weekday calls accepted
by professionals and non-
professionals; afterhour
calls picked up at hospi-
tals.

Columbus

Suicide Prevention Service
Columbus Area Community
Mental Health Center
275 E. State St. Tel. (614)
221-5445
24-hour service with professional staff. Daytime calls
are received at the center
and handled by staff; balance of calls are transferred to home of profes-
sional by answering ser-
vice.

Dayton

Suicide Prevention Center
137 N. Main St. Tel. (513)
224-1677
24-hour telephone answering
service, staffed by professionals. Answering service
refers calls to person on
duty; professional continues or refers to community
agencies.

Toledo

Rescue, Inc.
1933 Speilbusch Ave. Tel.
(419) 479-2773
24-hour telephone counseling service. A clergyman

answers calls with professional backup service.

OKLAHOMA

Tulsa
Suicide Prevention Center
1120 S. Utica. Tel. (918) 583-3355
24-hour answering service with nonprofessional volunteers and professional backup. Referrals to community agencies.

OREGON

Corvallis
Crisis Service
Benton County Mental Health Clinic
127 N. Sixth St. (503) 752-7030
24-hour service, weekday calls answered by clinic; other hours, professional and nonprofessional volunteers receive calls from answering service. Referrals to appropriate agency; clinic has professional resources.

Portland
Suicide Prevention Service, Inc.
P. O. Box 443. Tel. (503) 227-0403
24-hour telephone answering service staffed by professional and nonprofessional volunteeers.

PENNSYLVANIA

Bethlehem
Life Line (Bethlehem Area Council of Churches)
520 E. Broad St. Tel. (215) 691-0660
24-hour telephone service based at local ambulance service. Volunteers, backed by professionals and General Hospital Emergency service.

Philadelphia
Suicide Prevention Center
430 City Hall Annex. Tel. (215) 686-4420
24-hour service staffed by professionals. Daytime evaluation and referral service to community agencies when necessary.

TENNESSEE

Chattanooga
Suicide Prevention Service
Chattanooga Psychiatric Clinic
1028 E. Third St. Tel. (615) 698-7809
24-hour telephone service. Weekday calls are received and handled by the clinic; night watch handles balance of calls. Volunteers are professional and nonprofessional.

Knoxville
Suicide Prevention Association
Tel. (615) 525-2882
24-hour answering service by trained volunteers consisting primarily of professionals and ministers.

Nashville
Crisis Call Center (Nashville Suicide Prevention Service)
814 Church St. Tel. (615) 244-7444
24-hour answering service. Staffed with trained volunteers with professional backup. Referrals to other agencies where indicated.

TEXAS

Abilene
Abilene Suicide Prevention Service
610 Mims Bldg. Tel. (915) 673-3132
24-hour telephone service; trained volunteers.

Amarillo
Suicide Prevention-Crisis Intervention Center
2200 W. Seventh St. Tel. (806) 376-4251 or 376-4442
24-hour answering service with nonprofessional volunteers backed up by professional volunteers and clergymen. Referrals to community agencies.

Austin
Emergency Counseling and Referral Service
University Counseling Center, The University of Texas. Tel. (512) 471-3515
24-hour telephone service with semiprofessionals trained in psychology and related fields assisting in all emergency services.

Beaumont
Suicide Rescue, Inc.
330 Liberty St. Tel. (713) 833-2311
24-hour telephone service with referrals to community agencies. Staffed by nonprofessional volunteers with professional backup.

Corpus Christi
Suicide Prevention, Inc.
P.O. Box 3075. Tel. (512) 883-6244
24-hour telephone answering service with volunteers covering calls; professional backup and referrals to appropriate community agencies.

Dallas
Suicide Prevention of Dallas, Inc.
3615 Routh. Tel. (214) 521-5531

24-hour telephone answering
service. Staffed with
trained volunteers.

Fort Worth
Suicide Prevention of Tar-
rant County, Inc.
1300 W. Cannon St. Tel.
(817) 336-3355
24-hour telephone answering
service uses volunteers
with backup of profes-
sionals from the commu-
nity. Referral service.

San Antonio
San Antonio Suicide Prevention Center, Inc.
P.O. Box 10192. Tel. (512)
533-8550
24-hour service with professionals and nonprofessionals.

Waco
Suicide Prevention Program
of Waco and McLennan
County
1200 Lewis St.

UTAH

Salt Lake City
Salt Lake City Community
Mental Health Center
156 Westminister Ave. Tel.
(801) 484-8761

WASHINGTON

Bremerton
Crisis Clinic
Sixth and Marion Sts. Tel.
(206) 373-2402
24-hour answering service

operated by professional
and nonprofessional staff;
psychiatric and psycho-
logical consultants; referrals to community agen-
cies.

Olympia
Emotional Crisis Service
Community Mental Health
Center
1801 E. Fourth Ave. Tel.
(206) 357-3681
24-hour service with calls
being handled during
work week by Center;
at other hours the answering service relays calls to
home of professional.
Some home visits are
made when family needs
assistance with arrange-
ments for patient.

Seattle
Crisis Clinc, Inc.
905 E. Columbia. Tel. (206)
325-5550
24-hour answering service
with a volunteer returning
calls to person calling;
professional backup.
Multireferral service.

WISCONSIN

Eau Claire
Suicide Prevention Center
Psychiatric Unit, Lutheran
Hospital
310 Chestnut St. Tel. (715)
834-5522

24-hour telephone service staffed by registered nurses. Referrals made to community agencies when necessary.

Madison

Emergency Mental Health and Suicide Prevention Services

Dane County Mental Health Center

1030 Milton St. Tel. (608) 267-6234

24-hour emergency telephone service. Professional staff.

Milwaukee

Psychiatric Emergency Service

Diagnostic and Treatment Center

8700 W. Wisconsin Ave.

Tel. (414) 258-2040 and 258-2222

24-hour telephone and walk-in service. Staffed by professionals and nonprofessionals in day hours, and by professional residents after 8 P.M. Consultations, brief treatment and/or transfer to other Center units or community services. Sponsored by Milwaukee County Mental Health Center.

Elkhorn

Walworth County Mental Health Center

P.O. Box 290. Tel. (414) 245-5011

24-hour emergency telephone answering service. Professional staff.

18

Retirement and Aging*

Eternal God, teach us to number our days in order that we may have a heart of wisdom. Yet free us from undue anxiety and preoccupation with the need to remain young, to worship the idol of our younger years. Enable us to participate in the fullness of our years with courage; fill these years with meaning and fresh new sources of hope, and grant unto us the joys of deeper discoveries of friendship with others and with thee in our later years. Through Jesus Christ, who is the same yesterday, today, and forever, we pray. Amen.

In the 1970 census there were recorded nearly 20,000,-000 persons over the age of sixty-five. There are 135 older women to every 100 older men. Most older men are married, while most older women are widows, single, or divorced. In this age group, there are almost four times as many widows as widowers. This points to a reemphasis of the Christian concern for the care of widows as well as concern for the care of the aging and the aged. Seven out of ten older persons live in families. The remainder of them live alone or with nonrelatives. Only one in

* We are indebted to Herman Green, then Chaplain at the Masonic Home for Widows and Orphans, and now a staff member of the Family Life Department of the Sunday School Board of the Southern Baptist Convention for much of this data.

twenty lives in an institution. Three times as many older women live alone or with nonrelatives as older men. From an economic point of view, older families average just under half the income of younger families. Older persons living alone or with nonrelatives average only two fifths of the income of their younger counterparts. Almost 30 percent of the older families had incomes of less than $3,000 in 1968, and more than 40 percent of the older persons living alone or with relatives had incomes of less than $1,500.

When we identify the distinctly human factors in the facts just reported, several stand out clearly: *Loneliness*. Especially is this true of loneliness in women's lives in the later years inasmuch as women live longer than do men. *Poverty*. The incomes of older persons tend to be fixed, they themselves can do little or nothing about increasing their incomes, and they are living, in the main, below the poverty level of existence. *Dependence*. A considerable number of older persons are dependent upon their younger relatives, who have to add to the care of their own younger children the care of aging persons in their family in the context of a society that has decreasingly less need for the productive work of an older person. This was and is less true in a distinctly rural setting than an industrial-business-urban setting. *Hopelessness*. In a world in which a person is measured too often by the amount of goods he can produce, the amount of money he can make, and these become goals for his life, the sources of hope are cut off when these reasons for being are taken away. These are the real enemies that the aging person has to fight while his health declines and his or her fellow soldiers in the fight, his or her friends of many years, drop off by death. Where can you go for help?

YOUR CHURCH

This is the day for "nonnegotiable demands" from first one group and then the other. The older people of a church need to make a few demands for a place in the life of the church, one that is adapted to their life-style. Departments of ministry, departments of family life, etc., at the denominational and interdenominational levels have developed suggestions for local churches, but very little is done by the local church until the older persons themselves insist on programs for persons who are retired. Many churches already have extensive programs of involvement for older persons, and our experience has been that they got started by self-conscious effort on the part of the older persons themselves, aided and abetted by the pastor and younger persons.

YOUR GOVERNMENT

Extensive help and understanding is available from state and federal government sources. Every state except Wyoming has a State Agency on Aging. For example, Kentucky has the Commission on Aging, 207 Holmes Street, Frankfort, Ky. 40601.

The Older Americans Act Programs under Titles III, IV, and V provide services such as the Foster Grandparent Program, Retired Senior Volunteer Program, homemaker or home health aide services, home maintenance service, placement in foster homes, protective service, home-delivered hot meals, health screening and services, employment referrals, counseling, transportation service, recreation and leisure activities, adult education classes, special short-term training, and areawide model projects.

The Training Grants Program under title of the Older Americans Act supports fifteen long-term programs, offered in seventeen universities, to prepare students for careers in eighteen different occupational areas. These careers include community organization, federal-state planning and administration, recreational leadership, retirement-housing management, senior-center direction, administration of homes for the aged, adult education, counseling, architecture, business administration, communication, dental hygiene, health education, library science, speech correction, and urban planning.

For example, the fourteen-week residential institutes at the University of Michigan—Wayne State University —provide students, usually mid-career workers, with competencies in the areas of retirement-housing management, preparation for retirement, milieu therapy in the mental hospital, senior-center direction, and program administration.

Another example is the ten-day residential program conducted at the Pennsylvania State University to help ministers achieve a broader understanding of older people and a knowledge of community services for them.

Information on the training grants programs may be obtained by writing directly to the Editor of *Aging*, Administration on Aging, U.S. Department of Health, Education, and Welfare, Washington, D.C. 20201. (The above material came from *Aging*, May, 1970, Reprint No. 187, pp. 3–14, U.S. Department of Health, Education, and Welfare, Administration on Aging, Washington, D.C., U.S. Government Printing Office.)

SOCIAL SECURITY

Contact the Social Security Administration in whatever city or county you live in order to find specific information.

Qualifications for Social Security are as follows:

1. A person must have worked under Social Security for a certain number of three-month periods, called "quarters," which vary in number according to one's date of birth, and whether one is male or female.
2. The wife or widow of a man who has worked under Social Security is eligible.
3. A wife has to be sixty-two before she can draw on her husband's Social Security.
4. A widow who is sixty can draw reduced benefits from her husband's Social Security.
5. If a woman worked under Social Security, she can draw it on herself.
6. A woman who was seventy-two or over in 1968 and has no other income can draw Social Security.

Benefits have basic minimums that are from time to time increased by Congressional action.

NURSING HOMES

Chronological age in a human being is as deceptive as the year model of an automobile. The mileage, the way the car has been driven, by *whom* the car has been driven, and for what purposes the car was used make all the difference! Our human body is much like this. These differences show up—regardless of chronological age—in

204

the health of a person. In this respect, older persons fall into three groups: the healthy and vigorous, those with chronic disorders that do not disable but only limit, and the bedfast and infirm. The person with a chronic disorder, such as some types of arthritis, diabetes, etc., should, of course, maintain close contact with a physician, either on a private basis or through a local clinic. The big issue comes when a person needs more nursing attention than his relatives can provide without breaking their own home and health down. This is a new day of the professional nursing home. The professional home can help and should be considered. A fine pamphlet discussing aging and health is *Health Aspects of Aging*, published by the American Medical Association, 535 North Dearborn Street, Chicago, Ill. 60610.

Three kinds of nursing-home care are needed and are being set up to meet federal requirements for Medicare and Medicaid.

1. Nursing Homes. These homes care for the ill, injured, and infirm who need help below the intensity offered by a hospital, but help nevertheless delivered by professional hands. The home must have at least one registered nurse or licensed practical nurse on duty at all times. Most states require that nursing homes be licensed by the state Health Department. The price range at this time is usually $6 a day ($175 a month) to nearly $25 a day ($720 a month).

2. Intermediate-Care Homes. This level of care is just now being tried. It will provide care above the personal-care home, but below the care in a nursing home. Thus, limited nursing care would be pro-

vided, with nursing care available part of the time. The cost would be about $10 a day. Some nursing homes are setting up wings for this kind of care.

3. Personal-Care Homes. These are often called retirement homes. They care for the aged and infirm who usually can move about on their own but need someone to look after them. These people do not need nursing care. Personal-care homes are usually licensed. In Kentucky, they are licensed by the Department of Economic Security. The cost of care in these homes runs from $5 to $10 a day.

Another type of home that cares for the elderly is the Family-Care Home. These homes are often called "mini-homes." They are private homes that essentially offer room and board, but frequently nudge over into the area of nursing care. Public assistance in Kentucky and Indiana for older people in these homes runs from $100 to $200 a month.

Many private organizations, such as the Masons and the Eastern Star, religious denominations, and individual churches are providing some level of care for the elderly. Most of the homes are available only to members of the underwriting organization. However, some church homes maintain open membership, with no restriction on race, color, or creed, but with preference given to members of that church or denomination. This is done in order to qualify as an institution for building loans and grants, or patient-care financial aid (Medicaid) through local, state, and federal programs.

A person is eligible if sixty-five years or older, of good character, and in reasonably good health. Nursing-care facilities are available in some of these institutions, but a nursing-care patient may or may not be accepted. Emergency cases are usually not accepted out of fairness to those applicants on the waiting lists.

The cost of becoming a life-care resident in one of these private institutions usually requires that the older person donate all assets to the institution (including insurance and Medicare provisions). The institution in turn promises to provide a home and care for the remainder of the resident's life. Some allowance is usually given to the resident so that he will not be penniless. A certain percent of those older individuals whose assets will not meet the institutional cost of their care are usually accepted.

Some examples in the Kentucky area are:

The Masonic Widows and Orphans Home, Masonic Home, Ky. This home accepts widows of Masons from the age of sixty on up. It has a large nursing-care facility and does accept nursing-care patients.

Old Masons' Home, Shelbyville, Ky. This home accepts Masons and their wives from the age of sixty.

The United Church Homes. Operated by the Ohio Conference and the Indiana-Kentucky Conference of the United Church of Christ. It has five homes at the present time. Its membership is open, with no restrictions on race, color, or creed.

NATIONAL COUNCIL OF SENIOR CITIZENS

The National Council of Senior Citizens was formed as a result of the White House Conference on Aging, January 9–12, 1961. It was formally established in Detroit, Mich., during July, 1961. The Council offers information, leadership, and guidance through its publications. *Senior Citizens News* is published by the National Council of

Senior Citizens, Inc., 1627 K Street, N.W., Washington, D.C. 20006.

This organization is dedicated to making life better for all Americans, including the elderly. It is a nonprofit, non-partisan organization dedicated to social action on behalf of the poor and low-income elderly. In 1971 it conducted a membership drive for 5,000 affiliated senior citizens clubs with 5,000,000 members, including 1,000,000 with gold-tinted cards denoting direct affiliation with the National Council.

Gold Card members can take advantage of the following benefits:

1. Buy prescription drugs through the National Council's Direct Drug Service.

2. Sign up for the National Council's Medicare supplemental health insurance plan, which pays for many of the things Medicare does not pay (at a cost of $50 a year) or for life insurance available up to age eighty-five.

3. Take advantage of travel bargains offered by the National Council's Travel Department.

4. Gold Card members automatically receive *Senior Citizens News* delivered by mail to their homes.

The NCSC was a major factor in the passage in Congress of Medicare, the federal health-insurance program for persons age sixty-five or over, combined with Medicaid, the expanded Kerr-Mills federal-state health program for the needy. This bill was signed by President Johnson on July 30, 1965. The NCSC has also worked hard for the Social Security benefit increases in recent years.

The NCSC is now working for federal funds to assure an adequate level of living for the low-income elderly; removal of the Medicare out-of-the pocket charges for hospital, medical, and nursing-home care; extension of Medicare to out-of-hospital drugs; housing within the means of the low-income elderly; and consumer-protection legislation. Further, the Medicare Alert program of the NCSC is working to provide community-service jobs for the needy elderly to help them augment their inadequate incomes.

In a new project, the NCSC has just recommended that pharmacies be required publicly to post prices for all common prescription sizes of the most frequently prescribed drugs and to charge all customer-patients the posted price. (*Senior Citizen News*, Vol. 3, No. 112 [Washington, D.C., Dec., 1970], pp. 1–6).

THE AMERICAN ASSOCIATION OF RETIRED PEOPLE

The American Association of Retired People is another association that has many benefits for retired persons and persons anticipating retirement soon. These benefits include a subscription to its magazine, *Modern Maturity*, published bimonthly; research; counseling; correspondence; AARP Insurance Plan; AARP Pharmacy Service; and AARP Travel Service. For a small annual membership fee, the member receives *Modern Maturity*, as well as the monthly *AARP News Bulletin* and information on how to take advantage of the services of the Association. AARP works to secure fair treatment for people fifty-five or over, either actively employed, semiretired, or retired, and enters into research for ways to improve retirement conditions. The address is 1225 Connecticut Avenue, N.W., Washington, D.C. 20036.

A Reading List on Aging

Books

Beatty, Ralph P., *The Senior Citizen*. Charles C Thomas, Publisher, 1962. This is a good book for general information on the senior citizen.

Brown, J. Paul, *Counseling with Senior Citizens*. Prentice-Hall, Inc., 1967. This is in the Successful Pastoral Counseling Series. It is a good book for the minister who works with the aged.

Gray, Robert, and Moberg, David O., *The Church and the Older Person*. Wm. B. Eerdmans Publishing Company, 1962. This book is on the place and function of religion in the lives of older persons. It provides a good overview for the church to understand the needs of the older person, and it has some specific suggestions.

Hooper, Langdon, and McWilliams, Paul (eds.), *The Care of the Nursing Home Patient*. Little, Brown and Company, 1967. This is a good book for the minister, chaplain, nurse's aid, or family that has someone in a nursing home.

Kobb, Thomas, B., *The Bonus Years*. Judson Press, 1968. This is an excellent book for the minister and the local church to use in providing the resources to understand and meet the needs of older persons.

Poe, William D., *The Old Person in Your Home*. Charles Scribner's Sons, 1969. This is a very readable book for the family of an older person.

Pamphlets

The American Medical Association has the following
   pamphlets that can be ordered from them at 535 North
   Dearborn Street, Chicago, Ill. 60610:
   Employment of Older People
   How the Older Person Can Get the Most Out of Living
   A New Concept of Aging
   Stay Young, Think Young
Tell Me Where to Turn. Public Affairs Pamphlet No. 428.
   Public Affairs Committee, 381 Park Avenue, South,
   New York, N.Y. 10016. There is also a film by the same
   title that goes with the pamphlet. The AFL-CIO in
   Louisville has a copy of the film to loan or rent.

Periodicals

Oliva W. Coulter. *Aging,* ed. by U.S. Department of
   Health, Education, and Welfare, U.S. Government
   Printing office. John B. Martin is chairman of the Commission on Aging. *Aging* has been published since
   1951. Subscriptions should be addressed to Superintendent of Documents, Washington, D.C. 20402.
Geriatric Care. Ken Eymonn, Editor-Publisher. Published
   monthly for persons who work in institutions for the
   aged. For subscription information write: Geriatric
   Care, Drawer C, Loving Station, Minneapolis, Minn.
   55403. Tel. (612) 377-6855.
Journal of the American Geriatrics Society. Published by
   the American Geriatrics Society, Inc., 10 Columbus
   Circle, New York, N.Y. 10019. This is an excellent tech-

nical periodical for the geriatric doctor, but it has articles on psychology and sociology as well as on physiology that the minister can read and learn from. The same can be said for *The Gerontologist* and *Geriatrics*.

19

When Death Comes

O God, our Father, who art the God of the living,
we thank thee that we have eternal life in Jesus
Christ. We thank thee that nothing can separate
us from thee, neither life nor death, nor things
present nor things to come. We ask for a clear
awareness of thy presence in the shadow of death
in order that we may fear no evil. Lead us to
those who have suffered grief, who have faced
the threat of death themselves and who have received thy comfort in times of perplexity and the
temptation of despair. With the strength with
which thou hast comforted them, enable them to
comfort us. We need them and thee in this hour
of the great transition of life that we call death.
Through him who is the resurrection and the life,
Jesus Christ our Lord, we pray. Amen.

You are fortunate indeed if this is the first time that
you have either lost someone by death or had to face the
possibility that you yourself might soon die. Yet, if it is
not the first time this has happened, you are "acquainted
with grief" and death is no stranger. Many of us come
near to death one or more times before we actually die.
Therefore, if you have had such a time, simply recalling
how you "came through" will help you to be more con-

siderate of the real situation a loved one of yours may be facing in the same situation if he or she is on the verge of death. But more specifically, you yourself may be the one who is on the verge of death. You may be groping for some constructive way to think about your feelings and reluctant for one reason or another to talk with other people. A good private way of getting such a "conversation within yourself" going is to read one of the following books:

Mills, Liston O. (ed.), *Perspectives on Death*. Abingdon Press, 1969.

Ross, Elizabeth K. *On Death and Dying*. The Macmillan Company, 1969.

The person in your community who has more training and experience with persons facing death is your pastor. Often he himself may have suffered a great deal and can be better able to put himself in your place. Ask him to come to see you or to give you a time when you can go to see him.

Another suggestion is to live life to the fullest extent that your health will permit day by day. Jesus said that each day has enough trouble of its own. God will provide manna of strength day by day for you. No one of us can be sure of how long he or she will live. Before these lines are published one or the other or both of the authors *could* be dead in this very uncertain, hazardous world. Both you and we are alike in that we must live life the way it is given to us: a day at a time.

Again, do not be sentimental to the point that you deny your family the privilege of talking with you about your feelings concerning the short time that you have left to be with them. They can offset the loneliness and isolation that you feel and enable you to face death with dignity and strength. Let them give you a transfusion of courage.

However, you may be that family member whose loved one does "open up" to you his or her apprehension in facing death. You feel inadequate to converse with him or her. Remember that no one feels really adequate to do this. Everybody feels inadequate in talking about death, and much of our most meaningful conversation is nonverbal in touching, holding, and being near the loved one. However, the books we have recommended above will be especially helpful to the family member also who is called upon to minister to his or her loved one who is apparently dying. Bear in mind that you may be trying to protect your loved one from knowing his or her condition. Do not feel that you must tell them they are dying, because no one can be absolutely certain about this. However, give them an opportunity to tell you how they feel about themselves. Often it has been found that the person whose death is near will "know" as much about this as anybody else does. The facts, for instance, about cancer are just as available to them as they are to you.

You as a bereaved person will find yourself experiencing a new "installment" of grief as your loved one's condition worsens. The important thing to remember is that each hour of conscious awareness spent together is a precious treasure that should be spent carefully. Do not let the shortness of life obscure the depths that even a few minutes can reveal of eternal value and worth.

Then, regardless of how well you have braced yourself for it, when death finally comes you feel a deep shock. If it has been a long, lingering illness, do not feel guilty about the sense of relief you feel for your loved one and for yourself. Death is not just an enemy, but also a friend. The more sudden the death, the more shock you will experience. This will be followed by a period of numbness in which you will feel dazed. The practical tasks that have to be performed will help you to move ahead with life. They are specific. Do something specific. This will help you move through the next few hours and days. Do the following specific things:

SPECIFIC THINGS TO DO

1. Contact a funeral director or have someone do it for you, such as your doctor, a nurse in the hospital, the chaplain, your pastor, or a close friend or relative.

2. Make arrangements for your relatives to be notified. A pastoral ministry to them can be provided if you give a list of the names and locations to the chaplain of the hospital or to your pastor. Also, a close friend or relative can do this for you, but it is a specific thing that needs to be done.

3. Get the death certificate. This will be necessary for insurance purposes, the management of bank accounts, credit accounts that are insured, the establishing of eligibility for Social Security benefits, one of which is that a certain amount of money is available for funeral expenses from Social Security. Your doctor can advise you how to get the necessary copies of the death certificate.

4. Visit the funeral home and make arrangements for the funeral. The funeral director will show you three or four different price levels for caskets. Usually, the total funeral director's bill is a "package" with the price of the casket you select. Therefore, have this in mind before

you go into the conversation with the funeral director. A responsible funeral director will show you the four or five different price ranges he has to offer and let you decide how much you can spend. An unscrupulous one will not do this. If he does not, then ask, or even demand, that he do so.

At the same time you will need to select a grave plot if you have not previously done this. The funeral director will help in this matter. Again, he will show you the full price range for grave plots. If he does not, ask that he do so.

5. Ask your minister to help you arrange the order of service for the funeral. This can be planned entirely by the minister, or you can express specific requests for certain hymns, Scripture verses, and prayers. Most ministers are quite willing to have you tell them frankly whether you want a sermon or a eulogy in the service. The expressed wishes of the deceased for his funeral will be of great importance to you and to the minister in this planning. Tell the minister of any such wishes.

6. The funeral director and the minister together can help you in two final details—the selection of pallbearers and the writing of a notice for the local papers announcing the time and place of the funeral.

A relative or friend who is sufficiently composed emotionally can handle many of the details itemized above as something of a representative of your wishes. You might choose to "delegate" some of them and relieve yourself of the burden. You are normally depressed at such a time, and making decisions comes only with great effort. A wise friend or relative is a gift of God at such a time as this.

7. See your own doctor. It is important that you get

enough food, fluids, and sleep in order to get through this suffering with all the strength that your body has to offer. Your doctor can advise you medically how best to take care of your own health.

AFTER THE CROWD LEAVES

The feeling of emptiness in your life left by the death of your loved one begins to settle upon you when you return to your home. It takes full force when all the relatives leave and return to their homes. You must now take up life on your own.

At this time you will experience a real struggle between imagining that all this has not really happened and facing the hard fact that it has indeed happened. Your loved one *is* dead, but sometimes it does not seem so. The people with whom you do talk may be reluctant to discuss things about the dead person. You will need someone with whom to talk who is not afraid to do just this. Your pastor is a fine person to whom to turn. Another person who has lost someone by death is an excellent choice.

You will finally come to a point of "giving up and giving in" to the hard reality of your loss. You will then accept it. At this time you will feel like crying deeply again. Do it. It is "O.K." to cry. It is even good for a strong man to cry. Our Lord wept over his friend Lazarus, and you should pour out your tears also.

At about this time you may begin to look for something to read concerning grief. Get Granger E. Westberg's book, *Good Grief* (Fortress Press, 1971). Or read David K. Switzer's book, *The Dynamics of Grief* (Abingdon Press, 1970.) A woman who has lost her husband will find Catherine Marshall's book, *To Live Again* (Fawcett Publications, Inc., 1969), to be especially meaningful. Wayne E. Oates's *Anxiety in Christian Experience* (Waco, Texas: Word Books, 1971) has a brief discussion of the process of grief. The book of The Psalms is your best book to read. It is filled with a great variety of expressions of feelings that you will be experiencing. You will find, very quickly, passages that "speak to your condition."

You may have children who are also bereaved. It is important that they be permitted to see the corpse and go to the funeral if they wish, and allowed to talk about their grief. The minister of education in your church and your pastor will be especially interested in them. Two valuable books have been written to help you there:

Grollman, Earl A. (ed.), *Explaining Death to Children*. Beacon Press, Inc., 1967.
Jackson, Edgar, *Telling a Child About Death*. Channel Press, Inc., 1965.

Parents Without Partners, a very fine organization, has received nationwide attention and offers help to persons who are trying to be both mother and father to children. Its national headquarters are at 80 Fifth Avenue, New York, N.Y. 10017. You can contact this organization through your pastor, the Family and Children's Agency, or the central office of your United Appeal. These parents, with common problems, share with one another and also meet their needs to talk with other adults and not be reduced to talking only with children.

The last phase of the process of grief consists of discovering a new purpose and a new set of loyalties in life.

This does not mean that you are forsaking your love for your deceased loved one. It means that life has to go on, and new people enter your life to form new relationships that are loving in their own right. It means that life is lived forward and not backward. Memory enriches life, but hope is the stuff of which life itself is made. Hope is built upon satisfying present relationships and energizing future goals. There comes a time when we must let the dead bury the dead. Life must go on.

Index